CRITICAL ESSAYS
ON ROMAN LITERATURE

CONTRIBUTORS

W. S. Anderson
H. A. Mason
R. G. M. Nisbet
J. P. Sullivan

CRITICAL ESSAYS
ON
ROMAN LITERATURE

SATIRE

Edited by
J. P. SULLIVAN

ROUTLEDGE & KEGAN PAUL
London

First Published 1963
by Routledge & Kegan Paul Ltd
Broadway House, 68-74 Carter Lane
London, E.C.4
Reprinted 1970
Printed in Great Britain by
Redwood Press Limited
Trowbridge & London

SBN 7100 2163 1

CONTENTS

PREFACE

THIS volume of critical essays on Roman satire is a companion to
the first volume of essays on Roman elegy and lyric and is edited
on the same principles. Each of the contributors was simply
invited to submit a critical essay on their author and none of
them necessarily share any critical preconceptions. A difference of
tactics will be obvious to even the casual reader. This is perhaps
as it should be, for however favourable the atmosphere nowadays
to such critical attempts and however common and welcome the
appearance of such avowedly critical work, particularly in Ameri-
ca, the progress of this particular discipline within our studies has
been much slower than the older-established classical disciplines.
What progress there has been has been due largely to the efforts
of individual scholars and we have not seen anywhere the rise of
schools of criticism comparable to those in English studies and
most modern languages. Such schools have their disadvantages
as well as their advantages; but they do assure, in most cases, a
certain guidance for the individual who belongs to one of them
and provide that opportunity for discussion which is so important
for criticism. Perhaps the nearest thing to this has been the adoption by certain American scholars of the techniques of the New
Criticism and the current controversies about the proper method
of translating ancient authors. (It should perhaps be added here
that although translation can be a useful critical tool, the translations which are offered in this book of the Latin passages quoted
are meant, as before, simply for the guidance of the non-profes-
sional reader.)

This book is not intended as a substitute for a history of Roman
satire and only the major satirists make their appearance in it, for
I do not believe that we are in a position to make much of a
critical evaluation of the merits of Lucilius or Varro, although

vii

literary historians will no doubt continue to do what they can about this or what they imagine they can. Even in the case of the satirists whose work survives in sufficient bulk for an appraisal to be at least possible, the contributors have contented themselves with a minimum of historical background and information, both of which may be found more fully in such handbooks of Roman literature as H. J. Rose's *Handbook of Latin Literature* (1936) or Michael Grant's *Roman Literature* (1954).

The distribution of space to each of the authors discussed corresponds, I believe, to his relative importance to us. Juvenal is still for us the Roman satirist *par excellence* and Mr. Mason's essay is accordingly the longest. His more discursive critical approach may perhaps seem unusual to those accustomed to the more briskly direct methods of American critics, but the methods of comparison and analysis, the use of touchstones in the manner of Matthew Arnold, recommends itself more perhaps to English critics than to American. And the essay would, I believe, lose much of its critical persuasiveness and force were a different technique adopted.

J.P.S.

University of Texas
Austin, Texas

THE ROMAN SOCRATES:
HORACE AND HIS SATIRES

W. S. Anderson

THE Romans, according to the great rhetorician Quintilian, invented satire, and they generally agreed that the man who deserved the title of 'inventor' was Lucilius. Nevertheless, had not Lucilius been succeeded by Horace, who gave the rather amorphous poetry left by Lucilius an entirely new form, it is difficult to imagine how Roman satire would ever have developed a tradition and survived antiquity to exercise its marked influence on Renaissance literature. So important is Horace's place in the history of satire that one eminent scholar, G. L. Hendrickson, found reasons to describe Horace as the first to use the Latin word *satura* in a generic sense; that is, the first to give the modern literary meaning to *satura*. Although other scholars would date the literary use of the word earlier, Hendrickson correctly saw that Horace did revolutionize the whole field of satire. In what respects Horace was a revolutionary is the subject of this essay.

Lucilius, one of the last archaic poets, died just before the opening of the first century B.C. During the period of Horace's youth Lucilius' poetry was one of the most carefully studied bodies of verse available to budding poets. Not every reader caught the true spirit of Lucilian satire. Some thought that by imitating the savage invective with which the poet had assaulted eminent politicians of the Gracchan Age they were producing genuine 'satires'. We know of writers who lampooned the Triumvirs or who uttered polemic statements against personal foes; such writers, if they used verse, apparently claimed to follow the Lucilian model. However, the truly creative poets of the 60's and 50's, often called the Neoterics or New Poets, saw more clearly into the contribution of the older poet. His artfully stylized conversational manner, his ability to write verse with a strong personal stamp, his choice of ordinary subjects, his anti-heroic attitude, and finally his refusal to accept the political values of many aristocrats, all these made Lucilius' poetry one of the ideals of the New Poets.

Horace, born in 65, went to Rome as a boy to complete the education which he had commenced in his home town Venusia. Thanks to the advantages which his ambitious father secured for him, Horace would have studied Lucilius along with his schoolmates, sons of prominent senators. By the time he was a young man, he would have sensed the poetic trend which was gradually going beyond the Neoterics and their models. Another poet several years his senior, Vergil, published his *Eclogues* in 39; this work showed how far Roman literature had advanced from the Neoteric stage. Horace himself, shortly after the Battle of Philippi, had begun to compose his satiric verse. His efforts to chisel out a style and manner cost him much time, and it was not until 35 or 34 B.C. that he finally published a small body of ten *Sermones*, barely 1,000 verses. However, these 1,000 verses immediately proclaimed to the Roman world that Lucilius was challenged, if not superseded. The second great poet of the Augustan Age had appeared.

I. *The Socratic Style*

In his *Art of Poetry*, written long after 35, Horace cites as an especially fine model of correct writing the Socratic 'pages', those discourses of Plato, Xenophon, and other moralists of the fourth century B.C. which either presented the character of Socrates in action or used the same dialectic methods as he had once used.

> scribendi recte sapere est et principium et fons:
> rem tibi Socraticae poterunt ostendere chartae,
> verbaque provisam rem non invita sequentur. (*A.P.* 309–11)

The beginning and source of good writing is understanding: the Socratic pages will be able to indicate to you your matter, and, once you have determined your subject, the words will follow without difficulty.

It was familiar ancient doctrine, dear to the old Censor Cato, that the matter of a poem or speech came before its words. We do not think in that way any more, and it is pretty safe to say that Horace did not write that way. The very act of choosing words determines the meaning of a poem, often in a way quite different from the first poetic inspiration. Today, we would say that the words and the material of a poem cannot be separated and one element be regarded as prior in time and importance. Matter and words, form and content are inextricably related. Therefore, when Horace advocates Socratic content, we would not be surprised to learn that the accompanying words are also 'Socratic'.

G. C. Fiske showed more than forty years ago that Lucilius had created his satiric style in accordance with Stoic rhetorical doctrines. His Plain Style, a poetic version of the conversational manner, proved to be one of Lucilius' most influential innovations, and it affected not only satire but also, as I have said, the entire course of poetry in the first century. Nevertheless, when Horace decided to write satire in the modern style, he found Lucilius' version of the Plain Style altogether out of date. Struggling to define his own purposes, Horace could find no better way than to conduct a running polemic against Lucilius and his admirers. To put it at its simplest, Horace argued that Lucilius lacked the prerequisite of good writing, that understanding (*sapere, sapientia*), that self-discipline and conscious artistry which produces good poetry rather than witty anecdote or exciting invective.

To make his case effective, Horace emphasized one phase only of the double Lucilian tradition in the first century. While he virtually ignored the inspiration which his predecessor had given to great poets like Catullus, Horace concentrated on the invective poetry which Lucilius had also inspired. Thus, he characterized Lucilius by the Latin word *libertas*, using a pejorative sense of the word. No one English term can render all the meanings of *libertas*. Indeed, it took Horace himself a full poem to explore his idea of it (*S.* 1.4). Behind the noun, an abstract, lies the adjective *liber*, 'free'. The noun possesses all the possible meanings which 'being free' could have; it can refer to a noble freedom or a selfish irresponsibility. A Roman citizen, being free, could exercise certain political and social rights: he is not a slave. When one class interfered with the rights of another or when an individual tried to dominate Roman politics, the victims described this behaviour as an invasion of liberty. The political propaganda of the first century makes of *libertas* a passionate slogan. A secondary meaning followed on the first: if one asserted one's freedom by launching an invective against political foes, especially those that seemed to threaten one's rights, that was *libertas*. But a Roman citizen might display his freedom outside politics, especially this second sense of freedom. In his social intercourse he might be 'free' among friends of the same station. A true friend would express himself frankly and honestly, even when such freedom meant that he had to criticize a close companion; similarly, in the company of those he liked he would feel complete freedom to expose his deepest feelings. Lucilius represented himself as just such an honest friend. But since such freedom often took place in the setting of a banquet and at times degenerated into sheer licence, licentious remarks about others and unwise self-revelations; since also the Romans called the god of wine *Liber*, Horace deliberately associated *libertas* with the undisciplined and belligerent speech of a man under the influence of wine:

> saepe tribus lectis videas cenare quaternos,
> e quibus unus amet quavis aspergere cunctos
> praeter eum qui praebet aquam; post hunc quoque potus,
> condita cum verax aperit praecordia *Liber*.
> hic tibi comis et urbanus *liberque* videtur. (*S.* 1.4.86–90)

Often you can see four men dining on each of three couches, of whom one may like to bespatter with any sort of insult all the others except the host who provides the water; later, having drunk, the guest will insult the host, too, when truthful Bacchus discloses the secrets of his heart. To you, such a man seems genial, witty, and frank.

If we have not ourselves been drunk, we have seen drunks, and we all recognize the fact that Horace's picture of *libertas* is both prejudicial and accurate. It was meant to be so. While Horace rejects such drunken 'freedom', he refers to a person (*tibi*) who mistakenly values such liberty as both witty and amiable. This person, it seems clear, is thinking of Lucilius in these laudatory terms. And the satirist means us to see that Lucilius, the frank table companion, adopted an inadequate type of freedom. Ideally, the basis of freedom is a sense of responsibility, self-discipline which prevents one from interfering with the liberty of others. This besotted babbler—a caricature of Lucilius, I hasten to add—

violated all the rules of good manners so irresponsibly that he maligned his own host.

I shall return later to the moral problems which arise from Lucilius' use of *libertas*. For the present, I wish to consider how freedom, in the somewhat exaggerated picture provided us by Horace, affected Lucilian style; then I shall describe how Horace reformed this style in accordance with Classical principles. The passage which I cited from the *Art of Poetry* will afford us the critical term to define the Horatian manner: *sapere* or *sapientia*, understanding and conscious art, is the basis from which the Horatian satirist works and from which he expresses his disapproval of Lucilian freedom.

The drunken man has the unfortunate habit of cursing and slandering any and all people he knows; he also makes himself obnoxious by his long and incoherent monologues. If we listened to Horace, we would judge Lucilius to have been one of the most long-winded, incoherent, and undisciplined poets ever to have gained popularity; indeed, we would be surprised that Lucilius had won such favour with men of literary acumen. Yet Horace, at the very beginning of *S.* 1.4, closely connects with Lucilius' famous freedom of moral and political invective other less honourable traits: Lucilius constructed his verses crudely and heavily; he and his poetry flowed along muddily, with much material that an intelligent man would want to remove; he was garrulous and refused to tolerate the hard task of writing well (*scribendi recte*). Note how that last phrase, first proclaimed here as part of Horace's creed, remained a central part of his beliefs and hence recurred in the very passage of the *Art of Poetry* quoted above. The most vivid portion of Horace's description of Lucilius is a rapid sketch, almost a cartoon of the man:

> in hora saepe ducentos,
> ut magnum, versus dictabat stans pede in uno. (*S.* 1.4.9–10)

In a single hour, as if it were a great thing, Lucilius would dictate two hundred verses, standing on one foot.

Returning to this picture of Lucilian negligence in still another poem, Horace describes him as follows:

> ac si quis pedibus quid claudere senis,
> hoc tantum contentus, amet scripsisse ducentos
> ante cibum versus, totidem cenatus. (*S.* 1.10.59–61)

one who, content to enclose anything within the six feet of the hexameter, likes to have written two hundred verses before dinner and the same number afterwards.

Now, in Lucilius' time it was no crime to be able to dash off verse, especially for a banquet. Cicero, a warm admirer of Lucilius, himself took pride in his skill at composing verse rapidly. However, during the youth of Horace, the New Poets had attacked extemporaneous poetry and the cult of such versifiers; they demanded of the ideal poet absolute dedication to art. The small poem best answered their desires and most clearly represented the ideal of brevity and pungency which they insistently espoused; they extolled the poet Cinna for toiling nine years over his little epyllion entitled *Zmyrna*. Horace accepted these Neoteric principles. Throughout his *Sermones,* he mocks the facile Lucilius and his modern counterparts, fools who challenge the horrified Horace to a contest at extemporaneous versifying, fools like the man in *S.* 1.9 who really believes that the satirist will respect a man for contriving more verses more quickly than anyone else. To reform the incoherent chatter of Lucilius, then, this new satiric poet affirms as one of his basic tenets: *est brevitate opus* (*S.* 1.10.9). A poet must practise brevity.

Brevity characterizes Horatian satire from the smallest to the largest elements. In order to be more clear as to what Horace achieved, we should attempt to describe Lucilius' garrulity. Lucilius, a child of his times and therefore not at all averse to the mellifluous sound of repeated words or accumulated synonyms, showed a typical penchant for pairs and triads of synonyms. He used pronouns and conjunctions which would not be required by a reader a century later. Thus, glancing through his fragments, one gets the impression of a padded style, not spare and compact, but desultory and relaxed. In fact, it was the ideal style for the tone and character which Lucilius chose: his satirist was to be an urbane raconteur whose proper environment was the banquet. Horace, however, discarded this tone and this character, and consequently he consciously altered the style of his satire.

I shall not here attempt a detailed analysis of a Horatian passage to demonstrate the qualities of *brevitas.* Horatian satire is compact. The poet chooses his words carefully, so that one word, skilfully selected and emphatically placed in the verse, does the work of a whole Lucilian line. He tends to avoid synonyms, especially in a merely repetitive or emphatic function. When he uses pronouns, they count. Otherwise, pronouns, conjunctions, prepositions, in fact, anything that does not serve his Classical purposes are eliminated. Reading Horatian satire, then, is work. There are no moments for relaxation. Even the transitions from sentence to sentence often escape the casual reader, who suddenly finds himself in new territory, totally unable to explain how he got there. Brevity in phrase and sentence thus means that Horace can put more into his individual poems more effectively.

We can illustrate this effect of *brevitas* on entire poems by comparing two Satires, one of Lucilius' describing a journey to Sicily and Horace's *S.* 1.5, an account of a trip to Brundisium in the early 30's. According to the scholiast Porphyrio, Horace wrote his poem in part to vie with his predecessor and thus to demonstrate the clear superiority of the new satire. Of Lucilius' poem, there have survived some fifty lines, fragments never longer than four lines. Anyone who tries to piece these bits together must follow the evidence as far as it takes him, but inevitably he will resort to imagination; and differing views of the connexion between fragments have led to many varying reconstructions of the poem. However, despite all the variations, I feel safe in affirming that Lucilius' poem was considerably longer than Horace's. I would guess that it was between two and three hundred lines long, at least twice the size of Horace's poem of 104 verses. Lucilius described a private trip and the new sights and adventures that he had from day to day; what remains of his account has the character of a diary, with special entries on the number of miles from place to place, the type of lodging and food, and so on. It was a poem which must have been pleasant to listen to, which invited the comfortable, well-fed audience to picture the poor satirist toiling over rough roads, up and down mountains, tossing on the sea off Naples, taken advantage of by innkeepers and local prostitutes. In the satirist's diverting adventures a sensitive hearer could perceive an application to himself and all men, for this trip was symbolically no less than the journey through life, full of unpredictable changes, which must be faced with the same intelligent irony as shown by Lucilius' satirist.

Horace recognized the poetic merit of this theme. What he did was to compress and enrich the whole. He may give the illusion of writing a diary, but only an unobservant critic would be so obtuse as to call his poem 'a mere diary'. H. J. Musurillo has even urged a strong case for viewing the trip as a fiction. I myself tend to think that the trip probably took place, but that Horace so selectively recounted it that it has become a 'poetic fiction'. By compressing the details about mileage, terrain, and the like, Horace managed to give the full impression of a journey, without burdening the poem. He enriched the contents by making the expedition a collective trip of friends, all of them well known to his readers as prominent politicians and writers of the day. Whereas Lucilius pictured himself travelling to Sicily to attend to his estates, Horace attached his poem to an important political occasion. Maecenas has set out, accompanied by Horace, Vergil, Plotius, and Varius, to negotiate on behalf of the Triumvir Octavian with the emissaries of Antony and to make it possible for the two 'friends' to become reconciled. Momentous political events, then, are taking place, and the threat of war is very much alive; this time Antony and Octavian patched up their dispute, but the break was inevitable, destined to be settled a few years later at Actium. If a politician had recorded these events in a diary and then compiled his memoirs, we would have something like history, not a poem. The political events would have occupied the foreground, and Horace, nothing but a minor companion of the distinguished Maecenas, might have been listed as present, or again he might well have been ignored. Horace represents the episode from an entirely different perspective. The political crisis dwindles into the background, and instead the satirist and his friends, men of culture and humanity, take the front.

> postera lux oritur multo gratissima; namque
> Plotius et Varius Sinuessae Vergiliusque
> occurrunt, animae qualis neque candidiores
> terra tulit neque quis me sit devinctior alter.
> o qui complexus et gaudia quanta fuerunt!
> nil ego contulerim iucundo sanus amico. (1.5.39–44)

The next day dawns and is by far the most delightful; for Plotius, Varius, and Vergil meet us at Sinuessa. Never has the earth born more upright souls, and no man could be more bound to them than I am. O what embraces, what tremendous joy there was! While I am in my senses, I would compare nothing with the pleasure of friendship.

8

A slight Lucretian note pervades the poem, as if to suggest the Epicurean insight into reality, that the simple pleasures of life take precedence over blind ambition and political vanity. This satirist's ironic comments also have symbolic import. But while Lucilius' trip vaguely represented the ups and down of any life, Horace's trip dramatically faces his reader with urgent problems of the day and suggests a profound moral understanding of the relative value of politics and friends.

Lucilian *libertas* permitted the earlier poet to include within his poetry many topics which Horace, influenced by Neoteric tastes and Classical decorum, could not accept in his satire. Not only did Lucilius resort to synonyms and redundant pronouns, he also inclined towards language that would perhaps remind us of Rabelais because of its obscenity, sheer bombast, and delightful inventiveness. Lucilius regularly borrowed formidable compounds from Latin epic or created ridiculous ones of his own; and he was famous for his free use of Greek words, taken directly from Greek literature or slightly Latinized. This language fitted the exuberant genius of the poet and the tastes of his age, and it proved entirely congenial to the mask of the satirist. His racy language belonged to a man of wit, cultivated, intelligent, penetrating, but essentially more interested in displaying his cleverness than in pressing far into any moral or poetic problems.

From Horace's point of view, this exuberant satirist and his unrestrained witticisms, so manifest in his licentious language, had to be disciplined. True son of his age, which emphasized Classical ideals of balance, order, and self-restraint, Horace urged two important doctrines against Lucilius. First, the modern poet must adhere faithfully to *Latinitas*. By *Latinitas* Horace and his friends meant a good Latin style appropriate to an educated Roman citizen. Such a style would be free of provincialisms, of alien elements, of both vulgarity and preciosity. It had to fit the proprieties that had gradually been established for good Latin. Second, the poet should seek *concinnitas*. Cicero had long established the merits of *concinnitas* in rhetoric; the word includes within its meanings neat construction of a phrase or periodic sentence, harmonious balancing of ideas, elegant blending of words. Its common synonym is *elegantia*, a word that speaks for itself. Horace develops a persuasive argument in *S.* 1.10.20 ff in connexion with these two ideas, and, to do so, he uses a straw figure of an *adversarius* who praises Lucilius awkwardly and provokes crushing programmatic comments from the younger poet.

> 'at magnum fecit quod verbis Graeca Latinis
> miscuit.' o seri studiorum! quine putetis
> difficile et mirum, Rhodio quod Pitholeonti
> contigit? 'at sermo lingua concinnus utraque
> suavior, ut Chio nota si commixta Falerni est.'
> cum versus facias, te ipsum percontor, an et cum
> dura tibi peragenda rei sit causa Petilli?

Advers.—Lucilius really did a great thing when he blended Greek and Latin words.

Satirist—O what retarded standards! How in the world can you consider difficult or marvellous what comes by nature to the Rhodian Pitholeon [i.e. a foreigner]?

Advers.—But speech that is a smooth blend of each language is sweeter; it is like mixing the Falernian brand with Chian wine.

Satirist—Now I ask you, would you really hold to such an idea when you composed verse or when you had to conduct the arduous defense of Petillius in court?

By the time that he has dismissed this *adversarius*, Horace has clearly banned from his work all merely witty language, all outrageous vocabulary that suggests provincialism (such as that of a bilingual inhabitant of Southern Italy), and any Greek terms that have not long been at home in the Latin speech. Those who have amassed comparative statistics on Hellenisms in the *Sermones* have been able to demonstrate that Horace did precisely what he said he would: namely, he avoided violent borrowing of new Greek words, never constructed a Latin-Greek hybrid, and never quoted Greek at all. If, as I like to think of him, Horace modelled his satiric mask on Socrates, he definitely fitted himself into the Latin world as a *Roman* Socrates.

These three terms, *brevitas*, *Latinitas*, and *concinnitas*, have broader applications; but except for *brevitas* I have deliberately confined my attention to their immediate stylistic import, that is, to the way they direct the poet's selection of vocabulary. Now, suppose that a young Classical poet decided to adopt the Horatian criteria for satire. He would be most careful to be brief and pungent, to give the appearance of talking respectable Latin, and to have a sense of harmony. But where would he go from there? For example, what general tone or level of speech would he adopt?

The epic and tragic poets of Horace's age also accepted the three guiding rules which we have defined. Nevertheless, no writer of poetic satire would be mistaken for a tragedian or epic poet. Whereas the latter used what is called the Grand Style, the satiric poet, following the model of Lucilius, adopted the Plain or Low Style.

In general conception, the Plain Style in rhetoric and poetry aimed at an impression of conversation. I have repeatedly described the character of the Lucilian satirist as a witty dinner guest, well fed and moderately inspired by Bacchus, who delights others by his uninhibited discourse, sparkling with wit, gossip, anecdote, obscenity, political scandal, etc. Lucilius used several words to describe his poetry, but one particularly modest term which appealed to Horace was *sermo*; this means conversation. Horace does not call his poetic satires *Saturae* by way of title; instead, he calls them *Sermones*, discussions. The word *sermo*, then, defines the tone and range of Horace's satiric poems. As we shall see, the Horatian satirist does not assume the Lucilian mask, and therefore his brand of conversation differs markedly from the loose dinner remarks of his predecessor. Lucilian *libertas* yielded to Horatian and Classical *sapientia*.

While I have been using these rhetorical terms and simultaneously describing the writer of satire as a *poet*, the reader may have wondered what connexion there is. How does a conversational style become poetry? The answer to that question is not easy; it obviously bothered Horace himself. And yet unless we can answer it, we shall not really reach the true import of Horace's achievement. Anyone, with a moderate amount of effort, could summarize the Horatian moral philosophy, the Horatian attitude towards life, the Horatian outlook. Having done so, he would discover nothing especially novel. Horace is not an original thinker in his *Sermones*, and he does not pretend to be. It is so easy to parody his Golden Mean, for instance, that a teacher often finds himself embarrassed in commenting seriously upon it. The conclusion should be that, as in the case of most poetry, the heart of the poem is not the material discussed (as it would be prosaically summarized), but the way in which it is constructed and presented.

Horace plunges into a serious discussion in *S.* 1.4.39 ff in order to determine the place of his verse in the scale of literary forms. By associating satire with the more familiar Comedy, he is able to describe one type of verse that uses a simple conversational manner and to contrast it with the formal genres, best represented in Latin by Ennius' great epic, the *Annals*. If he were really as interested in Comedy as he affects to be, we would expect him to use the normal opposite of Comedy, that is, Tragedy. Rome boasted eminent tragedians in Ennius, Pacuvius, and Accius. But by choosing Ennius and epic poetry as his concrete antitype, Horace selects what is most precisely opposed to satire: epic is hexameter poetry on heroic topics in a noble style, satire is hexameter verse on mundane matters in a plain, everyday style. Thus, the true reason for linking satire with Comedy is probably that nobody really doubted the right of comedy to be called poetry. No sane critic would have denied that Plautus, Terence, or Caecilius were poets; he might have criticized them, but he had to treat them as poets. Similarly, while Horace seems to be asking and answering the question whether, in fact, satire and comedy can rightfully be defined as poetry, he is really endeavouring to describe the special poetic nature of the satiric style.

> primum ego me illorum dederim quibus esse poetas
> excerpam numero; neque enim concludere versum
> dixeris esse satis; neque si qui scribat uti nos
> sermoni propiora, putes hunc esse poetam.
> ingenium cui sit, cui mens divinior atque os
> magna sonaturum, des nominis huius honorem. (*S.* 1.4.39–44)

In the first place, I shall exclude myself from the number of those who I have conceded are poets; for you would not call it adequate merely to contrive a hexameter verse, nor, if anyone should write things more appropriate to everyday speech, as we do, would you consider him a poet. But if a man should possess genius, a particularly inspired mind, and a mouth able to pronounce great things, you would award this honorable name to him.

On the surface, Horace is contrasting grand poetry with his own slight genre. Taking an extreme position, he affirms that he is no 'poet', not at least in an important respect; he is not a grand poet. And for the moment he is willing to grant the title of poet only to the representatives of epic and tragedy. As if to emphasize the difference between *sermo* and epic, Horace does unorthodox things with his verse. In the first line he pushes three pronouns together with such apparent awkwardness that he has to elide *ego* and *me* and distort good prose and indeed poetic word-order. An elision of a monosyllable (*me*) reminds one of comedy and Lucilius; a collection of redundant pronouns was, we said, generally avoided by Horace, but typical of Lucilius. Horace also, for no good reason, reverses the order of *dederim* and *quibus*, and the consequent lack of elegance almost proves the sheer poetic incompetence of this *sermo*.

Now, looked at from a different side, these lines exhibit the special poetic possibilities of satire. Although the writer deals with a subtle argument, he explains his thoughts in simple language. Certain effects, like the personal pronouns, suggest the relaxed manner of conversation; yet at the same time they serve to emphasize the argument. By eliding both *ego* and *me*, Horace obliges us to feel the effacement of the lesser versifier by those august poets (*illorum*). Although he reverses the order of verb and relative pronoun and regularly removes verbs from their predictable prose position, Horace makes sure that important words are assigned to the key structual points of the hexameter. At the beginning of the line, the caesura, and the end of the line, he places words that count. Lucilius did not write like this, and this passage, like so many Horatian passages, reveals how a talented poet can conduct a reasonable argument and get the most out of his verse. Thus, we might say that Horace here proves how different *sermo* is from epic, but he also subtly shows that his own *sermo*, because it does so much more than imitate conversation, deserves the title of poetry.

As I said, Lucilius did not write like this. Thus, the brevity and clarity of the Horatian discussion acts as a commentary on the 'muddy' Lucilian manner. The implication of the passage seems to be that neither the interlocutor nor the poet would be content with such minimal achievements as contriving a verse and copying everyday speech, but that Lucilius was. The phrase *concludere versum* is pejorative in this context. Literally it means to enclose, confine, finish off a verse; but Horace alludes to the struggle which a mediocre versifier has in finding six metrical feet for the hexameter. I have already cited a passage, *S.* 1.10.59–61 (cf. p. 5), in which Horace turns this apparently general criticism precisely against Lucilius: Lucilius was a facile poet who was content to enclose anything within the six feet of the hexameter. Knowing what Horace does later, I think we can understand what he is more subtly doing here: while affecting to depreciate all satiric poets, he alludes pointedly to the man whom many contemporaries honoured as *Lucilius poeta*.

Lucilius, we are told by Horace, did regard it as a great thing that he could dash off two hundred hexameters on the spur of the moment. If any verse at all makes a poet, then Lucilius was a poet. But if a poet must be a craftsman, acting with insight and understanding, toiling and rewriting to get exactly the right touch, then Lucilius was no poet. Horace puts it another way a few lines later in *S.* 1.4. If you should take away the rhythm and meter and adjust the word-order slightly, Lucilius' verse would not retain a vestige of poetic quality; on the other hand, if you tried the same test on Ennius' *Annals*, you would still discover the elements of poetry in the disjointed fragments: *disiecti membra poetae* (62). In other words, Lucilius' verse was so intrinsically prosaic that, without the hexameter and its slightly distorted word-order, it possessed none of the virtues which Horace demanded in poetry. It is true that Horace includes himself together with Lucilius in this class of prosaic versifiers, but that is merely irony. His own verse belies him; he is master both of word-order and the hexameter.

The *Art of Poetry* contains a famous passage which we may confidently call one of the guiding principles of Horatian poetry:

> in verbis etiam tenuis cautusque serendis
> dixeris egregie, notum si callida verbum
> reddiderit iunctura novum. (46–48)

Again, modest and careful in sowing your words, you will have spoken better than most if a clever arrangement has made a familiar word new.

Everywhere in the *Sermones* an observant reader will find a *callida iunctura*, evidence that the poet has subjected his genius to rational scrutiny and made his words count. The word-order accomplishes much, and chiefly it contributes to the purposes of proper emphasis, ironic commentary, and economy. If one thinks of all the phrases which we owe to Horace, it is easy to see that their success depends on the fact that Horace chose the right words and placed them in the right order, with an inimitable skill; thus, *disiecti membra poetae* in *S.* 1.4. It simply is not true that Horatian Satires could be converted into prose without damage; my own reasonably exact translations should amply prove that.

The intellect which has limited the range of vocabulary, which strives for brief, precise statement of ideas, captures these ideas in the most lucid, reasonable, and artful style ever achieved in Roman satire. This ability to write such modest and yet so novel phrases was described by Petronius in the memorable words *curiosa felicitas*: he meant what we all soon observe, that Horace's signal felicity of expression depends upon the care which the poet used in selecting and arranging ordinary words.

Lucilius was no contemptible metrician. Before he chose the hexameter, he mastered the difficulties of two other meters, experimented with them as vehicles for his poetry, and discarded them. He knew exactly what he was doing in adopting the hexameter, and Horace's decision to follow in Lucilius' footsteps proves the value of the hexameter. Nevertheless, since the time of Lucilius, many poets had worked with that meter, and innovations and improvements made Lucilian verse seem heavy, crude, and slipshod. I shall not elaborate the details of Horace's changes; I merely wish to call attention to a few facts. Horace increases the dactylic quality of the line in accordance with contemporary tastes. He cuts down elisions, in particular elision of monosyllables. Above all, he gives the verse greater flexibility and movement by the dexterity with which he manipulates the caesurae and enjambement. Whereas much of Lucilian verse was end-stopped, Horatian conversation keeps on from one line into another, and the reader is drawn ever on into the discussion.

In conclusion, from these details, I would like the reader to gain an impression of a thoughtful conversational style. While Horace chose to caricature Lucilius by *libertas* (in a pejorative sense), he meant us to picture himself in an entirely different light. Irresponsibility and lack of artistic discipline marred Lucilian verse; total artistic discipline makes the Horatian style the monument of Classical poetry that it is. Yet I do not want to imply that the style should be viewed and savoured by itself. Horace criticizes Lucilius' irresponsibility in general, and Lucilius' talkativeness and refusal to work on his language and verse are merely symptoms of a general failure, in Horace's judgement. By the same token, the reasoned style of Horace, with its conversational basis, should serve to give us an impression of an un-Lucilian satirist, one whose reasoned conversation seeks not the immediate advantages of *libertas*, but the more permanent goal of *sapientia*.

This Socratic satirist will be the subject of consideration in the next section.

II. *The Socratic Moralist: Book I*

I have been talking so far about Horace's stylistic doctrines. I do *not* want to discuss Horace's moral theories or Horace as a moralist. My reason is quite simple: we do not know enough about Horace the moralist. There are details in the *Sermones* which biographical scholars have long taken as facts, but which a sceptic might legitimately question, and which in any case have been inserted to produce a certain impression for the immediate context. Musurillo has shown the logical inconsistencies in *S.* 1.5, and he doubts that Horace ever went on a diplomatic mission to Brundisium. The portrait of Horace's father, a composite of loving tributes in *S.* 1.4 and 6, raises difficulties. In the first place, Horace seems to be imitating Bion, a Greek forebear in diatribe. Secondly, Horace stresses the frugal simplicity of his father in such a way that one has difficulty in perceiving that, in fact, the elder Horace had a comfortable income. Again, the exceptional emphasis on the father has caused some people to wonder why Horace never once mentioned his mother. Not only does the portrait of the speaker acquire useful colour from these details, but Horace also makes sure that distracting facts do not mar or blur the picture. For example, we know from other sources that Horace studied a year or two in Athens, an opportunity enjoyed by only the most favoured young Romans. Yet he allows no such fact to enter the *Sermones*, for it might hurt the character of the commonsense moralist which is presented. After those few years of university education, Horace followed Brutus during the Civil Wars of 43–42 B.C., commanded a legion as a tribune, and fought at Philippi against the victorious forces of Antony and Octavian. Fifteen years later, in the Ode to Pompeius, he was able to look back on that battle and his flight with ironic amusement; at the time that he was writing his *Sermones* he could not discuss his recent political convictions. Therefore, his speaker affects complete lack of interest in politics.

It is important that we grasp this central feature of Horatian and all Roman satire: the speaker makes his criticism in the first person, and he presents himself as the poet, whether it be Lucilius, Horace, or Juvenal. In fact, this speaker is not fully identical with

the poet, no more than the impassioned lover is entirely identical
with the poet of elegy or lyric. In all personal poetry, the poet
assumes a mask, plays a part, and the role he takes may or may
not be very close to traits in his own personality. What we should
demand of the speaker is dramatic consistency; it is quite indifferent how far he copies the poet's career and feelings, but it is
absolutely essential that he should remain in character. When a
few years later Horace composed his Odes, he felt enterprising
enough to assume several quite different masks in different poems:
in one he is the inspired bard, in another the wistful, ageing lover,
in still another the moralistic preacher of intelligent enjoyment,
again the fiery patriot, the religious devotee, or the warm-hearted
friend. There are enough Odes so that these various characters
or masks all become familiar after a while. We know that Horace
published the nearly ninety poems of Books I–III in a group. On
the other hand, when he wrote the longer Satires, he did not want
any one of the ten poems in Book I to appear strikingly out of
character with the others. Accordingly, although he was in his
late twenties at the time of writing, although he certainly had
suffered in the social, political, and economic crisis of the Civil
Wars, and despite the fact that at that youthful age he must have
sought much feminine consolation, nevertheless, he strikes us as a
considerably older man, possessing the wisdom of experience,
serenely above the materialistic pursuits of his fellow men, capable
of a self-irony which only the profoundest self-restraint and self-
analysis will permit. How much effort must have gone into the
creation of that character by a young man not quite thirty, I leave
to the reader's imagination. The main point is that Horace produced a Socratic satirist probably quite unrepresentative of himself; and this satirist, the speaker in his *Sermones*, is one of the
greatest achievements of Horatian poetry.

I shall hereafter use the words 'the satirist' to refer to the speaker
in the Satires, as distinguished from his dramatic creator, the
satiric poet. In my usage, 'the satirist' will never be the real
Horace, and 'the satirist's' words, ideas, and behaviour will never
be assumed to be identical with those of Horace.

Horace did not invent this method of speaking through a mask
in satiric poetry. As a little reflection should indicate, the satirist
speaking in the first person is merely an extension of dramatic
and rhetorical practices long known, according to which any

actor or orator must assume the character appropriate to his speech. Rome produced the first elaborate personal poetry, and the first significant writer of personal poetry was Lucilius himself. Thus, Lucilius was the first to grapple with the problems of the mask in satire, and he showed the way to later poets in both elegy and satire. We have already discussed some of the more important aspects of Lucilius' satirist, particularly as they affected his style. All through the first century, during the time when Horace was acquiring his poetic tastes, his teachers and his fellow poets summarized the satirist in the single word *libertas*. While these critics felt no apparent need to distinguish Lucilius from his satirist, they did mentally draw the distinction. Varro used as a synonym for the licentious manner a significant phrase, *Lucilianus character*. The Latin *character*, based on the similar Greek word, does not yet possess all the connotations of our 'character', and I do not therefore mean that Varro's phrase precisely describes the *dramatic* role of the satirist. However, Varro did feel that Lucilius had stamped a certain personality upon his Satires and that that personality could be abstracted and discussed without reference to Lucilius' biography.

Today, we owe most of our impressions of Lucilius and his satirist to Horace. If we fail to differentiate Lucilius from his satirist, it is largely because Horace's polemic deliberately confuses the two. When, for example, Horace talks of Lucilius as garrulous or describes him writing two hundred verses on one foot or after a banquet, he is borrowing details from the Satires, spoken by or about the satirist, details which, in my opinion, are not fully applicable to Lucilius. One of the most sympathetic descriptions which Horace ever produces of Lucilius implicitly criticized the poet by confusing him with his satirist:

> me pedibus delectat claudere verba
> Lucili ritu, nostrum melioris utroque.
> ille velut fidis arcana sodalibus olim
> credebat libris, neque si male cesserat usquam
> decurrens alio, neque si bene; quo fit, ut omnis
> votiva pateat veluti descripta tabella
> vita senis. sequor hunc. (*S.* 2.1.28–34)

As for me, I take pleasure in (metrically) enclosing words according to the manner of Lucilius, the superior of us both. He once entrusted his secrets to his books as if to trustworthy companions, never running off anywhere whether things had gone badly or well; as a result, the whole existence of the old man lies open like a painted votive tablet. I follow in his footsteps.

While on the surface this appears to be a generous tribute to the first satiric poet, especially with its admission that Lucilius was 'better' than Horace or his companion Trebatius, below the surface runs the same series of charges against the slipshod and undisciplined Lucilius that Horace explicitly makes in Book I of the *Sermones*. Now, however, Horace does not use such pejorative adjectives as *garrulus, lutulentus, incompositus*; instead, he lets the criticism emerge from the description itself. Most of us have written diaries at some stage in our careers, in our youth when going through the throes of juvenile love or possibly during a trip to strange lands. We would be ashamed to let others, even our closest friends, peruse our indiscreet comments, because half the attraction of a diary lies in its permissiveness. We *can* indulge ourselves without fear of reproval so long as the diary remains secret. Now, Lucilius' satirist may have abused *libertas* to the point of indiscretion, but it does not necessarily follow that Lucilius himself was totally involved. Nor is it likely that Lucilius would publish all the facts about his own failures and evil intentions— we all have them—as Horace asserts. The satirist produced this impression of total revelation upon the reader, but Lucilius planned it that way. Therefore, when Horace compares the effect of Lucilius' Satires to that of a painted votive tablet, we may well wonder how far we should pursue the hints in the simile.

I vividly remember a visit I made about ten years ago to a little church in Marseilles. Inside it, covering the walls around the altar were the modern counterparts of the Roman votive tablets. I saw pictures of ships sinking (the most common topic of the Roman votary), trains bearing menacingly down upon tiny automobiles, of children about to race in front of speeding cars, all in garish colours and grotesquely dramatic gestures which testified to the anguish of the moment from which the Virgin had rescued the pious. This is art at the lowest level. The simple believer has no money to pay for a beautiful painting and usually lacks the taste or understanding even to wish for anything else. In that respect, Horace implies the inartistic picture produced by Lucilius. But it was also patently clear to Horace and his readers, who could visit shrines littered with wretched religious art or

who saw sailors on the street begging with the help of a melo-
dramatic painting of a shipwreck, that the votive tablet did *not*
correspond to reality. It was a poor version of life, distorted by
the incompetence of the artist and by his desire to concentrate all
attention upon a lurid, no doubt overemphasized tragedy. Now,
ancient critics had long since compared painting and poetry;
Horace uses this comparison as a prominent theme of his *Art of
Poetry*, indeed grasps the whole topic in his excellent phrase: *ut
pictura poesis*. Poetry is like painting, and poets should endeavour
to resemble superior painters. Good painters, as Horace knew,
reflected long on the way they would compose their picture and
what colours they would use. Similarly, he required of a poet
discretion and judgement, an ability to select and suppress, to
hint at facts briefly. The more the poet reflected, it seemed, the
better would be his rendering of the meaning of life. Thus, the
votive tablet representing Lucilius' poetry indicates first of all
the inartistry of that poet, but it also introduces the criterion by
which the satiric poet must be judged. He should be an artist and,
like a painter, depict an intelligible and coherent portrait, not a
luridly incompetent adventure.

The prevailing impression which, through Horace, we gain of
Lucilius is that of an excellent dinner companion. The great
Scipio Aemilianus and Laelius valued Lucilius' company, we are
told (*S.* 2.1.70 ff), and enjoyed gossiping and idly jesting with
him on the occasion of a banquet:

>   atqui
> primores populi arripuit populumque tributim,
> scilicet uni aequus virtuti atque eius amicis.
> quin ubi se a vulgo et scaena in secreta remorant
> virtus Scipiadae et mitis sapientia Laeli,
> nugari cum illo et discincti ludere donec
> decoqueretur holus soliti. (*S.* 2.1.68–74)

And yet Lucilius ripped away at the most important men and at the
people, tribe by tribe, of course fair to virtue alone and to virtue's
friends. However, when virtuous Scipio and gentle, wise Laelius had
retired from the mob and the public stage, they would regularly sport
with him and uninhibitedly play until the cabbage was cooked.

Those damning two hundred verses always appear, in Horace's
polemic, in the context of a *cena*; and when Horace alludes to
Lucilian wit, he usually manages to imply that this wit was stimu-

lated by wine. I infer from the near-uniformity of setting in which Horace conducts his polemic that Lucilius' satirist must have been typically presented either in a banquet scene or talking in a manner that was consistent with the *libertas* of the dinner table.

The virtues of such a satirist are relatively obvious: he seems friendly, amusing, frank, and confiding; he can talk seriously or lightly, but you yourself do not have to take him too seriously. Both Lucilius and Horace frequently employ the verb *ludere* and the noun *ludus* to define their methods, and we can profitably describe Lucilius' satirist as *lusor*, a playful individual. Horace treated the Lucilian satirist's virtues as negligible, or almost so, because in his opinion they were heavily outweighed by defects, all implicit in those words *lusor* and *libertas*. Balancing the slipshod style which Horace detected was a slipshod morality. At first reading, we might feel admiration for a satirist who never ran off to avoid describing both his good and evil (cf. the passage just cited). Second thoughts should suggest another interpretation. Take the verb *decurrens*: it can describe a person running, but it can also be used for a torrent running down a slope from the summit. Since Horace often uses the metaphor of the raging, muddy, uncontrolled torrent for Lucilius, this verb implies a typical Lucilian defect. He should have halted himself and not flowed on in the same heedless course regardless of content. For in Horace's opinion the satirist's *libertas* led him to impolitic and unethical comments.

Many people in Horace's youth reduced Lucilian *libertas* to mere invective. They recalled how the satirist had assailed a prominent triad of the late second century: Rutilius Lupus, Mucius Scaevola, and Metellus Macedonicus. I think it safe to say that Lucilius' satirist produced artistic and skilful political propaganda, but it also seems likely that it did impress readers as propaganda, written from the partisan perspective of the Scipionic Circle. That Horace disapproves of such attacks is more than obvious: he implies that the Lucilian satirist was half drunk when he assailed people. Sometimes, Lucilius' satirist took a more general position and attempted to reveal the contemptible and ridiculous behaviour of less distinguished people such as misers and spendthrifts (especially in the perspective of meals that they served) or foolish lovers. Having this intention, the satirist contented himself with a selection of pejorative details and epithets;

one of the most common adjectives in the surviving fragments is *improbus*, 'vicious', used as a label without adequate explanation. Again and again, the satirist branded a man of whom he disapproved as *improbus*, and the reader gains the impression that the attack on, and the exposure of, certain people entirely answered the satirist's purposes. For Horace, such a limited goal seemed merely one more defect of Lucilian *libertas*: the satirist of Horace, therefore, would not rest happy if he provoked laughter at the expense of some bitter victim. Finally, as *lusor*, the Lucilian satirist took a prominent, often dominant, part in certain amatory episodes. He was entirely in character when he described his attachment to Hymnis or Collyra and even when he adopted the role of *praeceptor amoris* and presumed to advise young lovers. However, Horace's satirist takes a more serious attitude towards life, and he refuses, except in *S.* 1.2, to entertain erotic ideas.

If one seeks a reasonably clear statement of the attitude of Horace's satirist, one does not have to read far in the opening Satire of Book I. Just after he has described the basic condition of human dissatisfaction, the satirist makes his transition as follows:

> praeterea ne sic, ut qui iocularia, ridens
> percurram—quamquam ridentem dicere verum
> quid vetat? ut pueris olim dant crustula blandi
> doctores, elementa velint ut discere prima;
> sed tamen amoto quaeramus seria ludo—
> ille gravem duro terram qui vertit aratro . . . (*S.* 1.1.23–8)

Furthermore, not to run over these matters laughingly, like a man running through his jests—although what prevents a man who laughs from telling the truth? Just as sometimes teachers give cookies to their young pupils as a bribe so that they will be willing to learn the alphabet; however, let us put aside our playing and seek the serious—that man who turns up the heavy earth with his hard plough . . .

Prepared as we are, we can read these lines with something like the background of the Roman audience and recognize the allusions to Lucilius. Horace's satirist discards *iocularia* and mere *ludus* as inadequate to his purpose, for he really begins his satiric development where the Lucilian satirist presumably left off. He intends to be serious, that is, morally serious. No doubt many people have heard that Horatian phrase *ridentem dicere verum* and thought of it as a summary of Horace's satirist. So long as we know the context in which the phrase originally appeared, we can use those words to summarize the satirist. However, if we should interpret those words apart from their context, we might be tempted to think that the laugh with which the satirist told the truth was a sardonic one, or we might guess that the 'truth' seen by the satirist was a partial, if not distorted, one. Then, the Horatian satirist would be no better than the Lucilian. But because we do have this context, we know that the Horatian satirist smilingly told a *serious moral* truth. Here is the principal distinction between the Lucilian and the Horatian manner: while the former is essentially *lusor*, the Horatian satirist is *doctor*. He is a teacher instructing puerile mankind in serious elementary moral truths, but willing to coax us by his laughing, ironic manner in order to impress his truths more effectively in our hearts.

Horace sets about depicting his satirist with the artistic skill that he apparently missed in Lucilius. Even in his arrangement of the poems in Book I, he tries to give a general impression of the satirist before letting the satirist speak about himself. The first three poems have the form of diatribes: the satirist discusses with an *adversarius* his conviction that avarice lies at the root of human dissatisfaction (*S.* 1.1), that our diverse sexual behaviour can be taken as the symbol of our moral self-punishment in general (*S.* 1.2), that self-indulgence and hypocrisy towards others undermine friendship (*S.* 1.3). Now, the diatribe had been created and much used by Greek popular philosophers, especially the Cynics and the Stoics, in the third century B.C. and thereafter. But it owed its origin to Socrates and the Socratic writers whom I cited at the beginning of this essay. In fact, as scholars have pointed out, diatribe is an approximate Greek equivalent of the Latin *sermo*, the title which Horace uses for his Satires. The Cynics and Stoics often took an overly righteous attitude and seemed to enjoy condemning the public in the harshest terms; we are familiar today with that method in the sermons of some revivalists, and Horace himself briefly describes, with ironic good humour, an arrogant Cynic at the end of *S.* 1.3. It becomes clear, however, that this satirist goes back beyond Lucilius and the Cynic-Stoics to Socrates himself for his model. He does not denounce; he does not unfairly ridicule; he does not triumph rhetorically over vice; he does not ignore his own failings. Like Socrates, he uses the disarming technique of discussion to force people to re-examine their consciences and to achieve a more rational attitude towards fundamental ethical problems.

Lucilius had devoted several poems to avarice and to amatory interests, and friendship served him as a constant sub-theme. Content to label the miser or lover as *improbus* and laughable, the Lucilian satirist made no explicit effort to instruct or to broaden his moral insights beyond the immediate problem. Therefore, to some readers, especially to those whom the satirist had picked out by name for ridicule, it seemed that Lucilian verse was *maledicus*, malicious and slanderous. Anyone reading Horace's first three poems would immediately catch the difference. This new satirist rarely fixes on a living person as an example, and never with animosity. He treats avarice carefully, trying to get at its basic implications. Then, he expands his argument and shows how avarice lies at the bottom of human unhappiness. Similarly, sex, which had been a playfully sensational topic in Lucilius, becomes in this satirist's hands a serious Epicurean problem bearing upon Man's predicament in life: he seeks *voluptas*, pleasure, irrationally and so inevitably incurs *dolor*, pain. Thus, the first three poems reveal a satirist who makes ethical inquiries into large, important human problems, discusses them calmly—with irony and not bluff ridicule—and makes them lead towards rational insights into ourselves and the moral order supporting the universe.

After these first three poems, in which we meet the satirist playing the role of the *doctor*, the Socratic inquirer using ordinary conversation to compel men to think about vital ethical questions, Horace placed three poems in which the satirist talks about himself and his personal convictions. *S.* 1.4, as we have seen, argues the new theory of *libertas*, responsible freedom and disciplined poetry. It ends with an appealing account of the satirist's father, who instructed the satirist in the use of moral examples and thus moulded his highly ethical use of specific people as illustrations. We have also seen how *S.* 1.5 provides the satirist an opportunity to contrast the meretricious goals of political ambition with the values of friendship and humane enjoyment. This attitude towards politics is explicitly proclaimed in *S.* 1.6: the satirist frankly admits his humble parentage—he is the son of a freed slave—and willingly relinquishes any right to engage in politics. Far more important to him are the friendship of Maecenas, the memory of an honest father, and the liberty of a disengaged life:

haec est
vita solutorum misera ambitione gravique;
his me consolor victurum suavius ac si
quaestor avus pater atque meus patruusque fuissent. (*S.* 1.6.128-31)

This is the life of men released from the wretched and heavy burden
of ambition. With such occupations I console myself, for I shall live
more pleasantly than if my grandfather, father, and uncle had all been
quaestors [i.e. attained political office whereby they automatically
became Senators].

S. 1.7 and 8 exhibit considerable wit, but the personality of the
satirist gains little from them. In *S.* 1.7, an anecdote of the Civil
War era is cleverly rendered; in *S.* 1.8, Priapus takes the place
of the satirist and gives a diverting tale of witches and how he
frightened them out of their senses. With the final two poems of
Book I, Horace takes up again the important themes of earlier
poems. As he was walking down the Sacred Way, recounts the
satirist in *S.* 1.9, a man came up to him and dogged his steps,
trying every method imaginable of gaining the satirist's favour
so as to secure an introduction to Maecenas, until fortuitously
another person appeared and snatched the first off to a law court
on some charge. In the encounter between satirist and the aggres-
sive individual, Horace dramatizes the conflict between the pre-
valent view of political goals (and of Maecenas' friends) and the
satirist's genuine desire to devote himself to his friends and
poetry. *S.* 1.10 reverts to the polemic of 1.4; its criticism of
Lucilius is more specific, and the satirist now invokes the literary
authority of Maecenas and his circle to guarantee his poetic merits.
As far as the satirist is concerned, the moral issues of *libertas*
received ample comment in the other nine poems, and he devotes
this final poem to an explicit defence of the status of satire, particularly Horatian satire, as poetry.

When a Roman thought about Socrates, he instinctively
thought of intelligent conversation on moral topics; then, he
might recall that Socrates surrounded himself with talented
friends, both literary men and politicians; or he might remember
stories about the utter simplicity and healthful nature of Socrates'
life. To this extent, the Horatian satirist feels completely in character. However, if the satirist had lacked another primary trait of
the famous Athenian, none of his other qualities would have
helped him in the least. That essential trait of Socratic discourse,

irony, is likewise an essential feature of Horatian discourse, and this guarantees his Socratic character.

The Romans valued irony, for they recognized how difficult it is to achieve the finest type of irony. Some scholars believe that Lucilius intended to achieve an ironic tone, and here and there some of his Satires do in fact lend themselves to such an interpretation. However, all too often the Lucilian satirist let his *libertas* proceed too far, and consequently his laughter became sardonic and mordant or mere jesting. Irony is intellectual; it smiles and avoids uproarious laughter. It uses humour where the tragedian uses pathos, to expose human failures, but always with a tinge of optimism. If we can understand the workings of such faults as political ambition, avarice, or sexual indulgence, and if we can be amused at the folly of those who do plunge into such faults, possibly we ourselves will be able to exercise our reason and so avoid similar error. For in the end all irony fails unless it ultimately is directed at oneself. Once we have understood ourselves and laughed or at least smiled at our mistakes, then we are entitled to express our amusement at others' mistakes. Our awareness of our own fallibility will make us more indulgent of others, less interested in the useless sport of exposing them to merciless ridicule.

We noted that the Horatian satirist rejected from the outset mere jests and foolery (*iocularia, ludus*) and yet approved of telling truth with a laugh: *ridentem dicere verum*. It takes little effort to perceive that this famous phrase summarizes the methods of Socratic irony. If we watch the irony at work in *S.* 1.1 or in the two other diatribes, we note how gently the satirist treats his *adversarius*. When the miser claims as his model the provident ant (1.1.33), the satirist does not sneer at his hypocrisy, as we might. Instead, he cleverly elaborates the points of difference between miser and ant and implies what may be the truth, that the miser is not so much hypocritical as unable to understand himself and his genuine motives. Thanks to this irony, the satirist really probes the truth, really enables us to understand the self-deception of the miser. When in *S.* 1.2 the satirist turns his attention to the mentality of the amorous male, he again shows us ironically that the real cause of our sexual difficulties resides not in our sexual instincts, but rather in our inability to subject them to rational inspection and control. The silly lover, for example, who thinks of love as a game and takes pleasure only in the pursuit of reluctant females (103 ff) stirs our amusement and helps us to see how irrational most sensual indulgence can be.

> 'leporem venator ut alta
> in nive sectetur, positum sic tangere nolit'
> cantat, et apponit 'meus est amor huic similis; nam
> transvolat in medio posita et fugientia captat.'
> hiscine versiculis speras tibi posse dolores
> atque aestus curasque gravis e pectore pelli? (1.2.105–10)

Lover (*lyrically*)—The hunter pursues the hare through deep snow, but refuses to touch the animal if within reach. My love is like that: for it flits past the available females and seeks to capture those who flee.

Satirist—And with trivial verse like that you hope that your pains and passions and your heavy lover's anguish can be driven from your heart?

To put it simply, Horatian irony is constructive, humane.

While the first three poems do use some self-irony, we can gain a clearer impression of its value by studying such 'personal' poems as 1.4, 5, 6, or 9. When in *S.* 1.5 the satirist concentrates on the sheerly mundane problems and pleasures of the trip to Brundisium and utterly ignores the momentous political discussions which occasioned the expedition, he is a master of irony. At first, we might take him for a man of no imagination, as we listen to his comments on poor food, eye trouble, a faithless prostitute, and the like. But gradually we see that such mundane crises and equally ordinary pleasures do make up the important part of human experience. The satirist's ability to look back upon this wearisome journey with pleasure and amusement reveals him as one who practices the Socratic virtues in his own existence.

In *S.* 1.6 the self-irony focuses on the satirist's admission that he is the son of a former emancipated slave. Another man would have regarded such an admission as a confession of weakness, and the satirist permits us to believe for a while that he, too, has been humbled. However, before the poem has ended, he boasts of his father and ironically proves that his simple, non-political form of life releases him from all sorts of miseries so that he can enjoy what really counts, namely, books, poetry, mild exercise, and friends. In other words, what the foolish regard as a grave disability, obscure birth, turns out to be the source of great moral strength. *S.* 1.9, like 1.5, lets the satirist recount an experience real or imaginary and, by his ironic reflections, reveal to us how a man with proper ethical standards should behave. Part of the irony depends upon a mock-epic vein that runs cleverly through the poem: the satirist suggests that his encounter with the political opportunist was a duel between two epic heroes. Unwilling to fight this opponent, the satirist wittily dramatizes his aversion to political engagements. On another level, the satirist shows himself too kind and sensitive to this insensitive man's feelings, and consequently he never says the one thing that would free him of his tormentor: a brutally frank 'Go away!' Again, he describes how his companion tries to ingratiate himself by boasting of an ability to write more verses faster than any Roman alive!

> 'si bene me novi non Viscum pluris amicum,
> non Varium facies: nam quis me scribere pluris
> aut citius possit versus? quis membra movere
> mollius? invideat quod et Hermogenes ego canto.' (1.9.22–25)

If I know myself well, you will not put a higher value on the friendship of Viscus or Varius. For who could write more verses and more quickly than I? Who could dance more delicately? Why, I can sing what even Hermogenes would envy.

What more ironic way could there be to appeal to the meticulous satirist, who weighs every word, toils over each verse, and constantly compresses his poetry into the narrowest effective scope?

The ironic manner, then, is the crucial means of instruction used by this Socratic satirist. Whether he assumes the role of *doctor* in the three diatribes or practises his own teaching in the later poems, he does constitute a positive model of behaviour which we can oppose to the series of deluded individuals who embrace some error to their ultimate sorrow. Essentially, he shows the contentedness available to a man who conducts his affairs by reason. Since the truth which he perceives is a complex one, he does not proclaim himself the saviour of mankind, nor does he sneer at others less intelligent than himself. Reason is the common possession of all men. If other men will utilize this special power, then they, too, can escape the materialistic and sensual commitments that have marred their lives. Hope exists for all men, provided that they use their understanding and look deeply into themselves as the satirist has done.

Book I of the *Sermones* marks a crucial stage in the development of Roman satire and of Horatian poetry. After studying Lucilius' very successful Satires, Horace decided on a thorough renovation. I assume that his primary interest was a poetic one. He set about to reform the style of satire, its tone, manner, and material. In opposition to Lucilian *libertas* he introduced Socratic *sapientia*. Such Socratic understanding demanded complete disciplining of vocabulary, exact choice of words, a delicate touch in word-order, and improvement of the metre; but the final product was what I call a Socratic style: an intelligent use of all the poetic materials available to the writer of verse satire in order to create an intellectual poetry. Yet this style did not exist by and for itself. Horace fully integrated it with his material, so that it is quite impossible to say that the contents followed on the style; the two go hand in hand. Thus, the intellectual style enables Horace to create his intellectual satirist, a modest and genial teacher (*doctor*), who shuns the cruder methods of Lucilius' playful and superficial satirist (*lusor*). As he serenely converses with misers, lovers, or Stoics in the early diatribes, or as he recounts his own convictions, based upon personal experience, this satirist makes it his business to tell the truth with a smile. If we grasp the import of that ironic truth, then we can achieve a balanced existence also. For this satirist is one of the clearest exponents of the Classical ideals which would become so dear to the Augustan Age. Thus Horace the poet forged a new style in Book I of the *Sermones* and created an entirely new satirist, a poetic achievement which for-ever dimmed the fame of Lucilius.

III. *Book II and the* Doctor Ineptus

Shortly after the Battle of Actium, apparently in 30 B.C., Horace published a second book of *Sermones*. These eight poems strike the reader as a further development away from the course set by Lucilius, and scholars today do not agree on the merits of this development. Some, like Fraenkel, argue that Horace went too far and so lost some essential virtues of satire; others feel that this second book reaches a poetic height that entirely justifies all its innovations. Fraenkel has shown how skilfully Horace borrowed from Plato in certain poems, and I wish to pursue the path which Fraenkel has indicated. In my opinion, the poetic genius of this book lies in its Platonic features.

It does not take one long to realize that the methods of conversation in Book II differ radically from those in Book I. We became accustomed to listening to the satirist in Book I, whether he argued serenely with some fictitious *adversarius* or recounted his experiences or stated his convictions about satiric poetry. The word *sermo*, as I showed, refers to conversation and can be regarded as in part equivalent to the Greek word *diatribe*. However, when Horace wrote Book I, he chose to let the satirist dominate the stage, and so, even where discussion takes place, the *adversarius* has no opportunity to elaborate his ideas and is confuted with ease by the didactic satirist. Opening Book II, we find ourselves in a strange world. The satirist lets himself be crowded off the stage by various fools who proclaim their warped ideas on various subjects, while the poor satirist meekly listens to them, uttering no criticism, often himself the target of misplaced ethical attack. It is as if we have plunged into a convincingly dramatic atmosphere, where the truth is no longer told, but is implied and awaits our investigation. The satirist's eminently intelligent discussion has yielded to a vividly erroneous discussion by someone other than the satirist; *sermo* has acquired a new sense.

The Socratic writings referred to in the *Art of Poetry* include the works of Xenophon and Plato which employed Socrates as a main character of dramatic dialogue. Xenophon admired Socrates as a teacher and attributed to him a didactic strain that may have been more Xenophontic than Socratic; his Socrates, at any rate, controls discussion and positively instructs all and sundry. I would suggest that the Socratic satirist in Book I bears a close resemblance to Xenophon's Socrates. Plato, who was both philosopher and dramatic poet, caught the spirit of Socrates differently. He typically wrote dialogues in which Socrates would be represented as ironically seeking instruction from someone else, asking questions which seemed easy but often led the other speaker to statements of manifest absurdity. Such dialogues frequently end without drawing any specific conclusion; Socrates does not state the philosophic truth, and we are left to resolve the problem with our own understanding, on the basis of what has been said. As I read the artful dramatic dialogues of Horace's Book II, it seems to me that I am expected to do precisely what Plato asks of his readers, to criticize the foolish speaker with my own rational faculties and thus to reach a clearer comprehension of the moral truth than the speaker possesses. Plato has found a successor who is at least worthy of him in poetic capacity.

The first four poems of Book II illustrate progressive stages of the Platonic development. In *S.* 2.1, because he feels troubled by hostile reactions to his work, the satirist consults his friend Trebatius as to what should be done. Trebatius gives various bits of solemn advice, but finally agrees that writing moderate satire may be a permissible occupation. Now, while I have summarized the general argument of the poem, I have not given an adequate impression of the dramatic dialogue. To understand the full import of the discussion it is necessary to grasp the character of Trebatius as here portrayed. Trebatius enjoyed the reputation of a prominent lawyer and friend of Caesar (soon to be hailed as Augustus). When consulted, therefore, he immediately assumes the habits of an attorney and gives serious legal advice to this satirist-client of his. Since Trebatius starts from the basic assumption that satire is a trashy, dangerous, and illegal type of poetry, the satirist really fails to communicate with him at all. On the one hand, Trebatius urgently prescribes behaviour that will avoid trouble with the Law; on the other hand, the satirist describes his understanding of the 'laws' of satire and how he endeavours to write good poetry within the bounds set by these 'laws'.

> 'sed tamen ut monitus caveas, ne forte negoti
> incutiat tibi quid sanctarum inscitia legum:
> si mala condiderit in quem quis carmina, ius est
> iudiciumque.' esto, si quis mala; sed bona si quis
> iudice condiderit laudatus Caesare? (2.1.80–84)

Trebatius—Nevertheless, be warned and see to it that you don't get into trouble through ignorance of the ordained laws, to wit: 'If anyone composes evil CARMINA against another, he is subject to trial and judgment.'

Satirist—All right, *if* they are evil. But suppose someone composed good CARMINA and was praised by Caesar the judge? [Trebatius' evil CARMINA are malicious incantations; the satirist's good CARMINA are poems of high quality.]

Against the background of the legalistic Trebatius' obtuse remarks, the satirist's confident grasp of his genre wins our smiling respect.

While in *S.* 2.1 the satirist does not attack Trebatius' statements,

31

nevertheless he does implicitly render Trebatius somewhat ridiculous. In *S.* 2.2, the advice comes from a character who does not differ entirely from the satirist; in fact, the satirist affects to repeat the doctrines of Ofellus, a man whom he respects. The early comments of the satirist, in which he disclaims personal responsibility for the doctrine, probably can be traced back to Plato's *Symposium*:

> nec meus hic sermo est, sed quae praecepit Ofellus
> rusticus, abnormis sapiens crassaque Minerva. (2.2.2–3)

And this is not my own discourse, but the precepts of Ofellus, the farmer, a homespun philosopher and man of rough intellect.

By denying responsibility for the following precepts and by describing Ofellus in this particular way, the satirist automatically sets up a conflict. For just as he could not follow the advice of the legalist Trebatius, it soon becomes apparent that neither he nor we can fully accept the harsh ways of Ofellus. This homespun philosopher sets out to harangue us on the merits of living modestly, and especially on the value of simple food. No sensible man would object to that purpose. However, in arguing his point Ofellus treats the gourmet with such contempt that we might, and should, feel his zeal excessive. Here, we could suspect, the satirist parts company with the man whose precepts he repeats. For in Book I the satirist adopted a more gentle attitude towards the mistaken, and he also described a less strenuous tenor of life on his part than Ofellus advocates. After all, our satirist is no self-taught farmer.

The satirist in *S.* 2.3 is sharply distinguished from Damasippus, the other character, who, in fact, dominates the conversation. To give the poem the fullest amount of dramatic irony, Horace sets the scene on the Saturnalia, which, like the old English Twelfth Night, was an occasion when fools played the master. The satirist has retired to his villa to avoid the riotous festivities and there, surrounded by his books (including Plato), he prepares to write his thoughtful poetry. Suddenly Damasippus bursts in, sneers at the slight merit of the satirist's poetic *sermo*, and proceeds to inflict upon the uncomfortable man a series of *praecepta* (34) that he has learned by heart from the wretched Stoic sage Stertinius. It seems that Damasippus had gone bankrupt in his antique business and, about to cast himself into the Tiber, was stopped by

Stertinius, who consoled him with the thought that not only Damasippus was crazy, but almost everyone else. Inspired by this dubiously profound thought and apparently forgetting that he himself is convicted of insanity, Damasippus launches into an interminable diatribe to demonstrate that all men tainted by avarice, ambition, luxury, or superstition are mad. The satirist asks one question: how does this apply to me? So Damasippus tries to convict the satirist of insanity, by the most extreme of charges, of which the last is that our mild little satirist feels passion for a thousand girls and a thousand boys! After all this ranting, the satirist makes his comment in a single verse:

> o maior tandem parcas, insane, minori!

O you who are a greater mad man, spare at last a lesser one!

Stoic extremism and the virtual hypocrisy of Damasippus thus tend to make the precepts of Stertinius suspect; they are not totally wrong, but they have been misused. A mute figure of reproach to impractical moral fanaticism, the satirist suffers the unreason of another without trying to correct him.

The opening of *S.* 2.4 might remind an educated reader of Plato's *Phaedrus* by its dramatic setting. As the satirist is calmly walking along, he encounters Catius, who appears in a great hurry. Questioned, Catius says that he is indeed pressed for time, since he wants to write down precepts that surpass those of Pythagoras, Socrates, and Plato. Such an extreme assertion naturally stirs the satirist's curiosity, and he pretends great eagerness, in order to persuade Catius to talk. Reluctantly, then, and with a fine show of condescension, Catius says: 'I shall sing these very precepts from memory' (11). As we soon discover, these *praecepta* directly oppose those voiced by Ofellus and Damasippus, for Catius is a gourmet inspired with strains of Lucretian enthusiasm to 'sing' an epic poem on the art of preparing a tasty meal for the perfect epicure. Scholars have convincingly shown that the recipes and dishes recommended by this didactic 'philosopher' do not violate good taste: they are not extravagant or exotic. Indeed, the reasonable satirist would be likely himself to partake of such food. However, because Catius exaggerates the value of preparing the ideal dinner into the proportions of an ethical philosophy, he exposes himself to criticism. But unless we ourselves have already determined the dramatic irony, the satirist's final remarks are lost on us:

at mihi cura
non mediocris inest, fontis ut adire remotos
atque haurire queam vitae praecepta beatae. (93–95)

'I am indeed most anxious to be able to approach those secret springs and to drink the precepts of the happy life.'

In pretending to share Catius' 'philosophic' interests and in parodying the Lucretian tone of Catius' inspired speech, the satirist maintains the irony to the very end.

I cannot here discuss all the eight poems of this book, but I hope that I have made the 'Platonic' trend more or less clear. Horace abandons the satirist of Book I, who endeared himself to us as a Socratic teacher. Instead, like Plato, Horace now constructs a truly dramatic dialogue and pushes the satirist into the supporting role, until by *S.* 2.4 the satirist does not even make a clear comment in opposition to Catius. In all four poems the satirist and we are obliged to listen to a series of slightly distorted precepts, whether they be Trebatius' irrelevant and learned disquisitions on the Law or the harsh rantings of the zealots Ofellus and Damasippus, each labelling as crazy all those who do not blindly accept their fanaticism. For the most part, the moral interpretation must come from our own poetic and rational insights, for even in *S.* 2.1, where the satirist presumably wants to argue the merits of his satire, he does so in such an ironic way that his best ideas usually escape the reader's attention. Perhaps we can make the distinction between Books I and II by describing the chief character (the man speaking to the virtually silent satirist) as a *doctor ineptus*. He is a teacher who fails to grasp the implications of his own precepts and thus ends as a figure of fun.

We described the ethical position of the Socratic satirist in Book I in terms of Classical balance: he did not condemn anyone utterly, but, urging the need for rational inquiry, tried to guide mistaken people from extreme error towards a modest happiness. To do so, he used his role as teacher to point out the misery suffered by those pursuing money, sexual gratification, ambition, and the like; or he described, by contrast, his own reasonable existence as a model of that happiness which he recommended. Now, except for one poem in Book II, the satirist has no opportunity to dominate the stage, and even that poem illustrates the different ethical method. Let us look briefly at *S*. 2.6.

As in *S*. 1.6, the satirist describes his happy life in contrast to the unfortunate pressures endured by the ambitious. But there is no argumentation, no effort to persuade us of a position. Instead, the whole poem works dramatically towards its end. We see the satirist in a moment of happiness on his Sabine farm. Next, he imagines himself plunged into the conflicts and tensions of Rome, where various people make unreasonable claims on him and envy him his close connexion with the influential Maecenas.

> per totum hoc tempus subiectior in diem et horam
> invidiae noster. ludos spectaverat una,
> luserat in campo: 'Fortunae filius!' omnes.
> frigidus a Rostris manat per compita rumor:
> quicumque obvius est me consulit: 'o bone, nam te
> scire, deos quoniam propius contingis, oportet,
> numquid de Dacis audisti?' nil equidem. 'ut tu
> semper eris derisor!' at omnes di exagitent me
> si quicquam. 'quid, militibus promissa Triquetra
> praedia Caesar an est Itala tellure daturus?'
> iurantem me scire nihil mirantur ut unum
> scilicet egregii mortalem altique silenti.
> perditur haec inter misero lux.

During this whole period, day by day, hour by hour, I have become increasingly exposed to envy. Suppose I watched the Games with Maecenas or played ball with him in the Campus Martius: everyone would call me a child of Fortune. Suppose a chill rumour seeps through the streets from the Rostra; then, whoever encounters me asks my advice. 'Good old Horace, you ought to know, since you practically touch the powers that be: what have you heard about the Dacians?' —Really nothing, I assure you.—'Oh, you will always joke, won't you?' —But I swear it; may all the gods drive me crazy if I have heard a word.—'Well, how about the land that Caesar promised to his veterans; is he going to allot it in Sicily or Italy?'—When I swear that I know nothing, they marvel at me as a unique specimen of extraordinary and profound taciturnity. This is the way I wretchedly waste my day.

Longing to escape from such misguided people, the satirist recalls with nostalgia the pleasant dinners which he would have in the country with his friends. At a typical banquet, Cervius might tell his fable of the Country and the City Mouse. It is with the satirist's version of Cervius' fable that the poem ends; and no final comment is permitted on the story. We may think of this fable as equivalent to the precepts of earlier speakers: it takes a moral stand, but we would be rash to identify the Country Mouse directly with our satirist. In fact, to make sure that we do not insist on absolute parallelism, the satirist describes the fable as a commentary on the anxious wealth of a certain Arellius (78). As I said before, the satirist is no farmer. He has retired to a small estate in the Sabine Hills which is worked by his servants; by contrast, the Country Mouse, like Ofellus, is a confirmed rustic, born and bred in the country and briefly lured to the city by his smooth-talking cousin. It remains for us to try to work out the relevance of the tale. According to my understanding of it, it serves as an ironic recommendation of rural contentment. The mouse fled from the Molossian hound and sought security in the country, resolved to accept its humble food as an inevitable consequence. The satirist longs for 'a delightful forgetfulness of the anxious life' (62), which cannot be achieved by flight alone, but primarily by an attitude of mind and heart. In itself, the country does not guarantee peace of mind; only after the satirist has controlled his acquisitive desires and his ambition does he find that charming oblivion that he associates with the rural landscape.

Thus, the poems of Book II demand a different response from our rational faculties, but they continue to demand rationality. No longer is our path marked out for us, as though all we had to do was to grasp the reasoning of the smiling Socratic teacher and follow his genial example. Now, between us and the 'truth' looms the opaque wall of dramatic irony. The *doctor ineptus*, whichever he may be, happily clings to his illusions and recites to the tolerant, but silent, satirist ideas which the speaker fondly believes to be glorious truth. However, as he launches enthusiastically into his 'precepts' the dramatic situation implies some inconsistency. This inconsistency, this dramatic irony is our means of breaking through to the truth. If we can see the difference between Damasippus' second-hand moral ideas and moral reality; if we can distinguish between true happiness and the culinary pleasures of Catius; then, perhaps, we may slowly work our ways towards that life of rational contentedness which the satirist still represents.

As I have indicated, many readers prefer the more direct appeal to reason that characterizes the Socratic satirist of Book I. I shall not attempt to prejudice the case by injecting my own preferences. Suffice it to say that the indirect manner of dramatic irony makes high demands on the poetic skill of Horace, who succeeds in assigning quite distinct characters to the various deluded 'teachers' in the eight poems. Moreover, Horace may come a little closer to the Classical spirit in Book II by leaving the truth undefined, dramatically indicated, and firmly believed, yet un-stated. But regardless of each reader's special likings, the fact remains that Horace's *Sermones* stand as a magnificent and early monument of the ideas and poetic art which best characterizes the Augustan Age. When Persius and Juvenal decided to write poetic satire they knew all too well that they were competing with a great poet; for in their thinking it is amply clear that Horace replaced Lucilius as the standard against which all later satiric poets would measure themselves.

PERSIUS

R. G. M. Nisbet

AULES PERSIUS died nineteen hundred years ago, on 24 November, A.D. 62: birthplace Volterra (Tuscany), rank equestrian, cause of death 'stomachi vitium', age 27. He left behind him six satires,[1] less than 700 lines in all, which were published by his friends and won immediate acclaim. Lucan testified that they were true poems, and whatever his faults, Lucan was a true poet. A less gifted but longer-lived contemporary, Quintilian, added his commendation many years later: *multum et verae gloriae quamvis uno libro Persius meruit* (10.1.94).[2] Though one has no great confidence in Quintilian's literary judgements (he preferred Tibullus to Propertius), it is worth knowing that at least in the ancient world Persius appealed to professorial taste. Persius's book was praised by Martial and imitated by Juvenal, and it was thought important and difficult enough to be dignified with a commentary. The grammarians referred to him freely, even Charisius and Diomedes, who did not quote Juvenal; evidently Persius was established in the educational curriculum sooner than his great successor. The Christian fathers copied him with gusto, and St. Jerome found a peculiar fascination in his forceful and contorted epigrams.

Persius's fame survived the collapse of civilization, and no Latin poet except Virgil can produce a more distinguished procession of witnesses to merit.[3] He was read and remembered by Cassiodorus, Isidore, Bede, and Heiric of Auxerre. His popularity between 900 and 1200 is attested by the entries in monastery catalogues and by the number of extant manuscripts: while authors like Catullus and Lucretius have come down by a single line, the pattern of Persius's tradition is so confused that it cannot be reconstructed in detail. In medieval England he is quoted by

William of Malmesbury, John of Salisbury, Walter Map, Roger Bacon; in renaissance Italy by Petrarch, Boccaccio, Laurentius Valla, Politian. In the sixteenth century he is imitated by Skelton, Wyatt, and Joseph Hall;[4] the hispid character of early English satire is partly due to a false assessment of his qualities. 'Lay her i' the earth,' says Laertes of Ophelia, 'and from her fair and unpolluted flesh let violets spring.' Though he did not know it, Shakespeare may have been influenced by Persius's sneer at the pretentious litterateur (1.39 f)

> nunc non e tumulo fortunataque favilla
> nascentur violae?

Now from his tomb and favoured ash will violets not be born?

At the beginning of the seventeenth century Persius was edited by the great Casaubon, who gave him first place among the satirists. He was imitated by Boileau, who sums him up in a judicious couplet:

> Perse en ses vers obscurs, mais serrés et pressans,
> Affecta d'enfermer moins de mots que de sens.

Dryden thought him worth comparing with Horace and Juvenal, and though his translation is for once unsuccessful, it at least confirms his interest and approval. In the eighteenth century Persius's influence diminished, but Gifford's *Baviad* is a close imitation of the first satire. The nineteenth century was on the whole unenthusiastic, though Renan made a curious exception. More recently Villeneuve[5] and Marmorale have tried to defend Persius; but their studies are so diffuse, and in the latter case so undiscriminating, that they have not received much attention. Persius is commended for his austere ideals in an impure age, and for his devotion to his mother, sister, and aunt. Candidates for university prizes read him, and some enjoy him. But relatively few scholars regard him as a poet, or think it possible that Lucan might have known what he was talking about.

Persius's satires are preceded (or in some manuscripts followed) by an epigram of fourteen lines, written not in hexameters like the rest, but in 'limping iambics'. They are of little importance in themselves, but they contain some typical satiric phrases, and they can be used to illustrate the vogue for our author in Tudor and Jacobean England. Persius begins by proclaiming that he never soused his lips in the horse's fountain, *nec fonte labra prolui caballino*: he means Hippocrene, but *caballus* (the ancestor of *cheval*) is a vulgar word. He never had a dream on two-headed Parnassus: this is a hit at Ennius, who claimed to have been visited by Homer during his sleep. Henry Fitzgeffrey catches the spirit of the thing at the end of his first satire (1617):

> It was nere my hap
> On high *Pernassus Top* to take a nap.

Persius leaves the daughters of Helicon and pallid Pirene to those whose busts are licked by the climbing ivy (*illis remitto quorum imagines lambunt / hederae sequaces*). Joseph Hall in the first satire of his *Virgidemiarum* (1598) attempts an indifferent paraphrase:

> *Trumpet, and reeds, and socks, and buskins fine*
> *I them bequeath* whose statues wandring twine
> Of Yvy, mixt with Bayes, circlen around
> Their living Temples likewise *Laurell-bound.*

Persius next asks himself his reason for writing:

> quis expedivit psittaco suum chaere
> picamque docuit nostra verba conari?

Who made the parrot so free with his 'hullo', and taught the magpie to venture human speech?

Skelton alludes to this passage in his enigmatic *Speke Parrot*:

> In Greeke tong Parrot can bothe speke and say,
> As Percyus, that poet, doth report of me,
> *Quis expedivit psittaco suum chaire?*

Persius answers his own question with a joke: it is the stomach which persuades parrots to talk and poets to write. These lines illustrate in a minor way two of our author's weaknesses. First, they are derived from books rather than experience: it was all very well for Horace to suggest that poverty had made him write, but Persius was a rich man. Secondly, the end of the prologue does not make a unity with the beginning. Some scholars have supposed that the poet's executors joined two fragments which they found in his papers, but such assumptions are unnecessary.

Persius was a slow writer, the ancient life tells us, and he had little gift for construction: his poems often leave us with the feeling that he has broken off for lunch in the middle.

The first satire also deals with the poet's reasons for writing, but here at least some serious comments are offered.

> o curas hominum! o quantum est in rebus inane!
> 'quis leget haec?' min tu istud ais? nemo hercule. 'nemo?'
> vel duo vel nemo. 'turpe et miserabile.' quare?
> ne mihi Polydamas et Troiades Labeonem
> praetulerint? nugae. . . . (1.1 ff)

The toils of men! The emptiness of life! 'Who's going to read that?' Are you talking to me? Nobody, of course. 'Nobody?' Well, two at the most. 'That's a poor show.' Why? Because Polydamas and the Trojan Women may prefer Labeo to me? Bosh.

The opening line is solemn and sententious, and there is no reason to doubt the scholiast's information that it comes from Lucilius, the father of Roman satire. There follows a snatch of conversation: the economy and verve of such passages are not sufficiently appreciated. The poet's friend puzzles modern readers, and Persius is blamed for not making him come to life. But that is to misunderstand the style. Such conversations are not really dramatic (Livy was wrong to connect satire with village plays); one should rather compare the orators with their 'Someone may say'. The trick was also used in Greek diatribe (popular philosophical discussion), which had great influence on satire. It is not always clear, nor does it matter, whether Persius is talking to himself or to somebody else. He is simply exploiting a lively rhetorical device to show the fluctuations of his thought.

The complicated and compressed allusions are also characteristic of our author. Polydamas in the Iliad is a symbol of respectability, who will reproach Hector if he falters; the Trojan Women are said by Homer to be equally censorious. Attius Labeo was a bad poet whose name has passed into English satire; Persius mentions him here, in the same context as Polydamas, because he translated the Iliad. This is an ingenious touch, but it does not compensate for the lack of precise criticism of Labeo's verse. Persius's satire would have more edge if he had abused distinct individuals for specific faults.

Polydamas can think what he likes, but Persius is indifferent to standards outside himself. This is doctrinaire Stoicism: in real life one supposes that he consulted his friends even more than Horace did. But he claims to have his secret reasons:

> nam Romae quis non—a, si fas dicere—sed fas
> tum cum ad canitiem et nostrum istud vivere triste
> aspexi ac nucibus facimus quaecumque relictis,
> cum sapimus patruos. tunc tunc—ignoscite (nolo,
> quid faciam?) sed sum petulanti splene—cachinno. (1.8 ff)

For at Rome who doesn't—ah, were it but permissible to speak—but it is permissible when I look at our venerable hairs and solemn lives, and then at all we have been doing since we gave up marbles, now that we have put on the airs of uncles. When I do that—I'm sorry, I don't mean to, I can't help it, it's just that I've a cheeky sense of humour—I cackle.

The lively parenthesis is typical of Persius: like Browning, he tries to reproduce the confused movement of thought and conversation, and again like Browning, he never lets the result sound quite like human speech. Editors who do not understand the style try to make *cachinno* a noun, meaning 'a jester'; but Housman, in his outstanding article[6] on Persius, exposed the futility of this interpretation. After his feverish apologies the poet finally produces a triumphant cackle, but he fails to reveal his deadly secret: that must wait till the end of the satire.

Persius now describes a recitation by a popular poet: such ceremonies had also annoyed Horace, but Persius has a sharper eye (though sometimes less feeling for atmosphere). The celebrity sits spruce in his high chair wearing a clean toga and his best ring; he has gargled his supple larynx with a liquid intonation (*liquido cum plasmate guttur / mobile conlueris*), and he ogles his audience disgustingly. William Gifford imitates the passage to describe Della Crusca reciting at Mrs. Piozzi's:

> So forth he steps, and with complacent air
> Bows round the circle, and assumes the chair:
> With lemonade he gargles first his throat,
> Then sweetly preludes to the liquid note. . . .
> A wild delirium round th' assembly flies;
> Unusual lustre shoots from Emma's eyes;
> Luxurious Arno drivels as he stands;
> And Anna frisks, and Laura claps her hands. (*Baviad,* 49 ff)

The lines are neat, but they have lost the energy of Persius's style: *plasma* is not lemonade or any other drink, but a rhetorical term for the modulation of the voice. Gifford never uses words in an original way: Persius does so repeatedly.

With a characteristic change of direction Persius allows the poetaster to put in a defence. It is one that is more common in the modern than the ancient world, the assertion that the creative impulse cannot be denied.

> 'quo didicisse, nisi hoc fermentum et quae semel intus
> innata est rupto iecore exierit caprificus?' (1.24 f)

'What's the use of study unless this frothing yeast and the sterile fig-tree, which has once taken root within, bursts the liver and shoots out?'

Other writers refer to the capacity of the growing fig-tree to burst the stones where it is lodged, but it took Persius to use the image with such bizarre ingenuity. Commentators say that 'the liver' means little more than the breast; they should rather compare Juvenal's words to the striving barrister: *rumpe miser tensum iecur*, 'strain your liver till it bursts'. Only Persius among Latin poets could have contrived so magnificent a mixture of metaphors. Such conflations are not regarded as an offence in Pindar or Shakespeare, so why in Latin?

But though Persius describes the urge to write so convincingly, he meets it with the stock, inadequate answer: 'Why publish?' He takes a lofty, unrealistic approach even to the desire for posthumous fame. Yet with his usual indecision he allows his opponent another word:

> 'rides' ait 'et nimis uncis
> naribus indulges. an erit qui velle recuset
> os populi meruisse et cedro digna locutus
> linquere nec scombros metuentia carmina nec tus?' (1.40 ff)

'You're laughing at me,' he says, 'and curling your nose too freely. Everybody must want to have earned a place on the nation's lips, and when he has said things worthy of moth-balls to leave poems that fear neither mackerel nor frankincense.'

In the first sentence Persius seems to combine four Horatian phrases, *rides ait, naso adunco, acutis naribus, naribus uti*. The third line parodies Virgil's '*Phoebo digna locuti*'. Again, Catullus had suggested that bad poems could be used for frying mackerel in, while Horace thought they would make pokes for incense;

Persius alludes to both with his usual economy.[7] H. E. Butler in his uncomprehending sketch[8] says that Horace became a veritable obsession with Persius, and that since he cannot keep Horace out he strives to disguise him. But Persius would have been very hurt if any of his cleverness had been missed.

Persius now admits that he is not indifferent to popularity (he is not made of horn), but he does deny that the ultimate test of excellence lies in the gushing exclamations of an emotional Italian audience. The prosperous patron of letters invites his struggling satellites to dinner, and then asks for candid appraisal of his work. Persius gives it to him: *nugaris cum tibi, calve | pinguis aqualiculus propenso sesquipede extet*, 'Your verses are light-weight, bald-head, though your fat pot-belly dangles out a foot and a half'. Then with magnificent grotesqueness he meditates on the fortune of two-headed Janus, who can never be criticized behind his back:

> o Iane, a tergo quem nulla ciconia pinsit
> nec manus auriculas imitari mobilis albas
> nec linguae quantum sitiat canis Apula tantae. (1.58 ff)

O Janus, whom no stork pecks behind, nor a hand deft at mimicking white ears, nor tongues big enough for an Apulian bitch's thirst.

These lines are sometimes criticized for obscurity; yet an ancient reader would have known that it was a rude gesture to imitate a stork's bill, or a donkey's ears, or to stick out one's tongue. *tantae* is undeniably feeble, and Barth's *tentae* ('stretched') deserves consideration;[9] it is not clear whether he intended it as a genitive singular or nominative plural. The emendation gains a little support from St. Jerome's characteristic adaptation (*Epist.* 125.18): 'si subito respexeris aut ciconiarum deprehendas post te colla curvari aut manu auriculas agitari asini aut aestuantem canis *protendi* linguam'.

The pretensions of the literary establishment are intolerable, but the poetry-loving public is just as bad. It thinks only of the smoothness of verses, and supposes that the technique of a modern poet is equal to anything. Fathers warn their sons to avoid old-fashioned tastes:

> 'est nunc Brisaei quem venosus liber Acci,
> sunt quos Pacuviusque et verrucosa moretur
> Antiopa aerumnis cor luctificabile fulta?' (1.76 ff)

'Is there anybody now who could pore over the shrivelled tome of Dionysian Accius, or Pacuvius and his warty Antiopa, whose dolorific heart resteth on tribulation?'

These lines form a question, and they give a point of view of which Persius disapproves. The description of Antiopa is perhaps the best parody in Latin. Most ancient parodies belong to the facile sort where an incongruous phrase is interpolated in a familiar quotation, but here Persius caricatures the oddity of the whole archaic style. Even if he has in mind a particular passage of Pacuvius, it would be a brilliant *tour de force* to reproduce it in a different metre.

Other parodies follow, this time of the moderns:

'cludere sic versum didicit "Berecyntius Attis"
et "qui caeruleum dirimebat Nerea delphin,"
sic "costam longo subduximus Appennino".' (1.93 ff)

'Thus "Berecyntian Attis" has learned to round off a line, and "the dolphin that clave sea-green Nereus", or "we have filched a rib from the long Apennines".'

Persius seems here to be scoffing at the Alexandrian tastes which survived in the early empire (witness the pseudo-Virgilian *Ciris*); the Greek mythology is too precious, the word-order of the second line is reminiscent of neoteric 'epyllion', and the spondaic ending *Appennino* is affected. Yet the point of the criticism partly eludes us, perhaps because some specific imitation is now lost.

The next words are also difficult.

' "Arma virum": nonne hoc spumosum et cortice pingui
ut ramale vetus vegrandi subere coctum?' (1.96 f)

' "Arms and the man": isn't this puffy stuff made of bloated bark like a desiccated branch baked with overgrown cork?'

Here the interrupter finds fault with the Aeneid for being out-of-date; such criticism now seems strange, but Seneca recognized in Virgil some clumsy and archaizing verses.[10] *spumosum* suggests dried scum rather than watery froth; the reader should imagine not soap-suds but a dried-up sponge. Some commentators assign the words to Persius rather than to the ghost-voice; they explain *arma virum* as an oath, and think that the satirist is contrasting the virile Virgil with the flaccid modern style. But the smooth

'Berecyntian Attis' could hardly be compared with a dried-up branch, and the lines that follow suggest that the interrupter is speaking.

The next parody is much easier:

> 'torva Mimalloneis inplerunt cornua bombis,
> et raptum vitulo caput ablatura superbo
> Bassaris et lyncem Maenas flexura corymbis
> euhion ingeminat, reparabilis adsonat echo.' (1.99 ff)

'They filled their grim horns with Bacchanal booms, and the Bassarid, like to tear the head from a prancing calf, and the Maenad, ready to rein a lynx with ivy-clusters, cry "Euhoe Euhoe" while the responsive echo chimes in.'

The scholiast assigns these lines to Nero, but he greatly exaggerates both Persius's audacity and his sense of relevance. The parody would hit off the facile fluency of many Silver Age poets (note the future participles, and the dactyls of the last line). Lucretius had lamented the poverty of his ancestral tongue, but now any trivial person could turn out slick Swinburnian hexameters without thinking what he was saying:

> summa delumbe saliva
> hoc natat in labris et in udo est Maenas et Attis
> nec pluteum caedit nec demorsos sapit ungues. (1.104 ff)

Dryden has the right idea:

> *Maenas* and *Atys* in the Mouth were bred;
> And never hatch'd within the lab'ring Head.
> No Blood, from bitten Nails, those Poems drew:
> But churn'd, like Spettle, from the Lips they flew.

'That may be so,' says the candid friend, 'but it is unwise to grate on sensitive ears with the tingling truth: *vide sis ne maiorum tibi forte/limina frigescant*', 'take care for my sake that the doorsteps of the great don't freeze for you'. Here the satirist once more is imitating Horace (*Sat.* 2.1.60 *maiorum ne quis amicus | frigore te feriat*), and once again he has improved on his model: doorsteps can be cold literally as well as metaphorically. Persius meets the interrupter's point by a conventional appeal to the invective of Lucilius (Horace and Juvenal do the same, though none of the three was in a position to write invective himself). He suggests that even Horace had made some valid criticisms of his friends and society:

> omne vafer vitium ridenti Flaccus amico
> tangit et admissus circum praecordia ludit,
> callidus excusso populum suspendere naso. (1.116 ff)

Sly Flaccus touches every fault of his smiling friend, and gaining admittance plays round his heart-strings, with a knack for balancing the crowd on his well-blown nose.

The characterization is brilliant: *vafer*, for instance, pictures Horace as a clever, ingratiating slave. Yet though Persius is so ingenious with his words, he does nothing about imitating Horace in practice.

The satirist now digs himself a hole, and breathes into it the deadly secret that he has been carrying since the beginning of the poem:

> hic tamen infodiam. vidi, vidi ipse, libelle:
> auriculas asini quis non habet? (1.120 f)

I'll bury it here. I saw I saw it, my book, with my own eyes: who hasn't got a donkey's ears?

The ancient biographer informs us that Persius originally wrote *auriculas asini Mida rex habet* ('King Midas has a donkey's ears'), and that the change was made after his death to avoid offending Nero. The story might have some truth in it, for it is easier to bury a statement than a question. The reading *quis non*, to be sure, is supported by *quis non* in l. 8; but it is just possible that l. 8 was changed as well. Persius's intentions were innocent: if he wrote 'Midas' he meant the word to symbolize pretentious people in general. Yet literary critics should not say that the emperor has no clothes at a time when the reigning emperor writes poetry.

Persius claims to be maintaining the traditions not only of satire but also of Old Comedy. Horace had seen a link between Lucilius and Aristophanes, and though the direct connexion was very remote, it is true that both indulged in personal invective. Persius professes to keep up the convention of his genre, but he does not, in fact, attack contemporaries: even the discreet Horace is more topical. The lack of invective is not, however, important; venomous self-righteousness can easily become boring. It is more serious that Persius offers little of the social comment which is found so abundantly in the comic poets.

Persius's final claim is more sensible. He is writing for the discriminating reader who likes *aliquid decoctius*, 'something boiled down': his own density of expression could not be more succinctly described. He does not write for people who sneer at Greek sandals and say 'One-eye' to a one-eyed man (Juvenal would have done both these things). Such persons think that they matter just because they are magistrates at Arezzo with the right to smash short measures: Juvenal borrowed this passage (10.101), for Persius was not the only satirist to imitate his predecessors. People like that can read the law-reports[11] in the morning and see a revue after lunch, but Persius does not want them for his admirers. The satire ends appropriately with a declaration of seriousness.

The second satire is written in honour of Macrinus's birthday.

> Hunc, Macrine, diem numera meliore lapillo
> qui tibi labentis apponit[12] candidus annos. (2.1 f)

Count this day, Macrinus, with a better pebble, the white day that credits to your account the gliding years.

The scholiast tells us that Macrinus belonged to the circle of Servilius Nonianus, and that he loved Persius like a son: this is not much to go on, and the poem says even less than this. Horace had used satire as a vehicle for the expression of friendship, and he liked to introduce small touches which suited a particular individual. Thus, in inviting Manlius Torquatus to supper, he offers him a wine from the battlefield of his most famous ancestor[13] (*Epist.* 1.5); and he tells Aristius Fuscus, who was a schoolmaster, not to let him go *incastigatum* or unchastised (*Epist.* 1.10). One finds none of this urbane banter in Persius. We may be told that Cornutus is a philosopher and Bassus a poet, but they remain as lifeless as Juvenal's Umbricius and Calvinus. Persius was not old or confident enough to write about himself and his friends; perhaps, too, his friends were rather dull. This was a pity: the personal element had been the most significant feature of Roman satire and was much more important than the invective of which the satirists themselves talk so much.

The subject of the second satire is the right and wrong types of prayer. The theme was a commonplace in philosophy and declamation, and editors quote parallels from Plato and Seneca; but the most instructive analogue is Juvenal's tenth satire, the 'Vanity of Human Wishes'. Juvenal wrote the more striking poem; his astonishing fertility of invention and his eye for the telling detail are nowhere seen to better advantage. By comparison Persius seems bald and perfunctory. Yet it should be remembered that in the second satire he may still have been feeling his way; the first is programmatic and unlikely to have been written first. In several ancient collections the second poem is demonstrably early (Virgil's *Eclogues*, Horace's *Satires* I and *Odes* I–III).

Macrinus is immediately forgotten and Persius turns to more serious matters. He begins with the iniquity of silent prayer.[14] Men may voice noble aspirations when somebody is listening, but soon they are muttering unavowable ambitions under their tongue:

> 'o si
> ebulliat patruus, praeclarum funus!' et 'o si
> sub rastro crepet argenti mihi seria dextro
> Hercule! pupillumve utinam, quem proximus heres
> inpello, expungam; nam et est scabiosus et acri
> bile tumet. Nerio iam tertia conditur uxor.' (2.9 ff)

'If only my uncle would pop off—a grand funeral'; and 'may a crock of silver thud under my spade by the grace of Hercules'; or 'if only I could chalk off my ward, who's doing me out of a legacy; he's got both scrofula and jaundice. Nerius is burying his third wife already'.

The string of commonplaces is paralleled in Horace and Petronius, but the idiom is original. The prayer for buried treasure is more conventional than convincing, but the thud of the pot is a vivid elaboration of Persius's own. The pensive aside on Nerius is deftly contrived: Persius should not be criticized here for abruptness, but complimented for observing the movement of thought.

To Persius such prayers are outrageous. If one avowed such ambitions to Staius he would say 'Good God': so why shouldn't God say 'Good God' himself? (*at sese non clamet Iuppiter ipse?*) Here Persius is being cynical, in the ancient sense of the term; that is to say, he is imitating the earnest irreverence of the followers of Diogenes. He continues in the same vein: 'Do you think you are let off because in a thunderstorm the oaks are split sooner than you? Just because you aren't lying in the woods with a fence round you to mark the spot, that doesn't mean that Jupiter is going to let you pull his beard. Do you think you have bought God's ears by a bribe of greasy intestines?' Roman satire did not have to be satirical in the modern sense, but it sometimes was; and Persius saw the possibilities of the style. In such derisive passages he is going farther than Horace and pointing the way to Juvenal.

There follows another conventional scene, the old woman's prayer for a baby's future fortune. Persius describes with cruel realism how she takes the child from his cot and smears her spittle over his brow. And then she prays:

> 'hunc optet generum rex et regina, puellae
> hunc rapiant, quidquid calcaverit hic rosa fiat.'
> ast ego nutrici non mando vota. negato,
> Iuppiter, haec illi, quamvis te albata rogarit. (2.37 ff)

'May a king and queen want him to marry their daughter; may girls scramble for him; wherever he treads may roses bloom.' But I don't delegate my prayers to a nurse: refuse her, o Lord, although she ask thee in her Sunday best.

The contempt is Stoic and seems cold to modern taste. Yet Juvenal is much worse: after describing a mother's prayers for her daughter's beauty he hints that she might be safer with a hunchback. Persius is never cynical that way.

Persius next discusses prayers for health and long life, but he exhausts the subject in three lines (contrast Juvenal's fluent treatment). It is foolish, he says, to pray for strength when our rich pickles stand in God's way; Diogenes the Cynic had said the same thing (Diogenes Laertius 6.28). Then back again to wealth: why pray that your cattle may prosper while your calves' guts liquefy in the sacrificial flame?

> et tamen hic extis et opimo vincere ferto
> intendit: 'iam crescit ager, iam crescit ovile,
> iam dabitur, iam iam' donec deceptus et exspes
> nequiquam fundo suspiret nummus in imo. (2.48 ff)

But all the same he tries to win his wish by means of animals' entrails and rich sacrificial-cakes: 'now my fields are growing, now my sheepfold, now I'll get my hands on it, now at any minute', until disappointed and despairing at the bottom of the money-box the last coin sighs unavailingly.

suspiret again shows Persius's remarkable gift for using language in a new and exciting way.

Another cynical touch follows: men cover the gods' images with a film of gold because they imagine them as avaricious as themselves. This leads to one of the most eloquent passages in Persius:

> o curvae in terris animae et caelestium inanis,
> quid iuvat hoc, templis nostros immittere mores
> et bona dis ex hac scelerata ducere pulpa? (2.61 ff)

Souls stooped on the ground and void of the divine, what use is it to introduce our own morals into the churches, and infer the gods' good from this sinful flesh?

In the solemn language of law and religion Persius asks the sacred college for a ruling: *dicite pontifices, in sancto quid facit aurum?*, 'what avails gold in consecrated ground?' We should offer something that bleary Messalinus could not give from his big platter: purity of heart and nobility of mind. One naturally compares Juvenal's concluding prayer for 'mens sana in corpore sano', but though Juvenal is more memorable, Persius is more convincing, both here and throughout the satire. Juvenal delights to demonstrate that achievement of one's hopes may lead to disaster; Persius is genuinely concerned with leading a good life. To Juvenal, Demosthenes and Cicero would have fared better if they had never become great orators; Persius may have a professional veneer of cynicism, but he is never cheap.

The third satire begins with one of the most vivid pictures in Persius:

> nempe haec adsidue. iam clarum mane fenestras
> intrat et angustas extendit lumine rimas.
> stertimus indomitum quod despumare Falernum
> sufficiat, quinta dum linea tangitur umbra.
> 'en quid agis? siccas insana canicula messes
> iam dudum coquit et patula pecus omne sub ulmo est'
> unus ait comitum. (3.1 ff)

Always the same story. Already the bright morning is coming through the shutters and widening the thin chinks with light. We are snoring enough to take the froth off fiery Falernian while the line is touched by the fifth shadow [i.e. it's 11 o'clock]. 'Here, what d'you think you're doing? The raving dogstar has long been baking the thirsty crops, and the whole herd is under the spreading elm.' So speaks a friend.

The scene that follows is equally convincing, especially to those who have found themselves in the same predicament. The sluggard takes hold of pen and parchment (which is suitably described as two-coloured, as the hair has been removed from one side). But nothing goes right. First the ink is too thick: it was one of the hazards of composition in antiquity that the author had to mix his own. Yet when the stuff is diluted, the pen can only make watery blobs.

> an tali studeam calamo? cui verba? quid istas
> succinis ambages? tibi luditur. effluis amens,
> contemnere. (3.19 ff)

How can I work with a pen like that? Who d'you think you're fooling? Why the snivelling about the bush? It's your move. You're heedlessly dripping away, and you'll soon be written off.

These racy lines show Persius at his best: the combination of earnestness and liveliness is individual and typical. He continues with his lecture: 'You're wasting your youth, the most impressionable time of your life. The man in the street may admire you because you belong to an equestrian Etruscan family, but I know what lies under your trappings. You are worse than Natta, for he has lost all sense of right and wrong, and has sunk so deep that he blows no bubbles on the surface (*et alto | demersus summa rursus non bullit in unda*).'

The drift is clear, but who are the *dramatis personae*? It used to be supposed that the sluggard was as shadowy as Natta, a mere dummy borrowed from diatribe and declamation. It was assumed that most of the opening scene was spoken by an anonymous friend of the anonymous sluggard. It is true that the first person plural *stertimus* (l. 3) does not usually mean 'you are snoring'; yet it was pointed out that modern doctors sometimes say 'How are we today?' However, in 1913 Housman exploded the prevailing explanation, and it can no longer be taken for granted that the bedside plural is a legitimate Latin construction. He showed that the whole opening passage (except 5–6) is spoken not by the candid friend but by the sluggard himself. And as for this mysterious personage, Housman observed what ought to have been noticed before: an earnest young man who writes slowly and comes from a prosperous Etruscan family can only be Persius.

Housman's solution has been distrusted by editors, with the

notable exception of Clausen, but it makes sense of the whole passage. The dialogue is conducted between the satirist's higher and lower selves; this suits the conventions of popular philosophy. It may be objected that the drunken stupor of l. 3 ill suits our virtuous author. But Persius does not say that he was drunk, only that his snores could have coped even with Falernian (the scholiast is right here; so is Dryden). Persius is certainly obscure, but not so obscure as some editors have made him.

Persius takes a serious view of his late start in the morning, and is led by it to some impressive moralizing.

> magne pater divum, saevos punire tyrannos
> haut alia ratione velis, cum dira libido
> moverit ingenium ferventi tincta veneno:
> virtutem videant intabescantque relicta. (3.35 ff)

Sir Thomas Wyatt imitated this passage at the end of his second satire, and caught the gravity of his original.

> None other pain pray I for theim to be
> > But when the rage doeth led theim from the right
> > That lowking backward, Vertue they may se
> Evyn as she is, so goodly fayre and bright;
> > And whilst they claspe their lustes in armes a crosse,
> > Graunt theim, goode Lorde, as thou maist of thy myght,
> > To frete inward for losing suche a losse.

But though Persius's words are fine, they come in rather abruptly. Hendrickson wished to transpose ll. 35–43 to follow 57;[15] yet any disjointedness should probably be ascribed to the satirist rather than to his executors. It can be explained by his lack of fluency and overconscientious methods of composition, but perhaps that is not the whole story. Certainly it is remarkable that similar jerkiness is found elsewhere in Stoic diatribe: Epictetus and Marcus Aurelius, as well as Persius, composed by the paragraph.

After this portentous interlude Persius resumes his lighter style with an unusually genial reminiscence from his schooldays. He tells us his embarrassment at having to learn up Cato's dying speech and then recite it in front of his perspiring father. So he smeared his eyes with olive oil, and by this simple stratagem persuaded his family that he needed a rest. It is surprising to find the impeccable Persius resorting to such devices, but he claims that his action was quite reasonable: when he was a child he knew no better. Backsliding is much more reprehensible now that he is a man; for now he has learned the lessons of 'the portico daubed with trousered Medes' (the facetious periphrasis for the Stoic school points the way to a stylistic mannerism of Juvenal's). Persius's argument shows Stoic unreasonableness at its worst, but one is grateful for the detail about his sweating father. There is only one snag, pointed out by Villeneuve:[16] Persius's father died when he was six. It is not very likely that his stepfather is meant, especially as he, too, died a few years later. The most personal anecdote in Persius seems to be a piece of fiction.

Persius now shifts his ground slightly. So far he has been blaming people who waste their lives in spite of having studied philosophy; now he suggests that philosophy may be of some help. He thinks that it can give protection against spiritual ailments before their onset; the medical metaphor is characteristic of popular moralizing. There follows a string of Stoic aphorisms which can be paralleled in Epictetus and Marcus Aurelius.

> discite et, o miseri, causas cognoscite rerum:
> quid sumus et quidnam victuri gignimur, . . .
> quem te deus esse
> iussit et humana qua parte locatus es in re. (3.66 f, 71 f)

Be instructed, miserable men, and learn the first cause of things: what we are, what sort of life we are sent into the world to lead, . . . what part God has ordered you to play and where you have been stationed in the commonwealth of human-kind.

After this impressive sermon Persius suddenly shifts his style: 'You mustn't ignore philosophy just because your larder is full of groceries presented by clients in the country.' The passage was imitated by Juvenal, but Juvenal never attempted so piquant a blend of diatribe and satire.

Next comes a digression in which a centurion makes unfriendly remarks on philosophy. Hendrickson acutely observes that the passage would be more appropriate at the end of the poem (cf. 1.127 ff, 5.189 ff); and it must be admitted that in spite of its cleverness this satire is very oddly arranged. The centurion claims to know what's what without outside assistance:

> non ego curo
> esse quod Arcesilas aerumnosique Solones
> obstipo capite et figentes lumine terram,
> murmura cum secum et rabiosa silentia rodunt
> atque exporrecto trutinantur verba labello.[17] (3.78 ff)

I don't want to be like Arcesilas or some careworn Solon, with their stooped heads and eyes nailed to the ground, while they gnaw mumbles to themselves and rabid silences, and weigh their words on outstretched lips.

Like all Persius's characters the centurion talks like Persius, just as Juvenal's characters talk like Juvenal; neither attempted the subtle variations of style which we find in Horace. But though dramatically unconvincing the lines are stylistically brilliant. Conventional critics are dismayed: nobody can literally gnaw mumbles, or for that matter silences. Yet if one takes a step back the phrase as a whole is wonderfully alive and not in the least obscure.

Persius now describes a sick man who in defiance of his doctor takes a heavy dinner and a hot bath. Editors seem puzzled by the sequence of thought, but the passage is simply a parable, as Dryden in fact saw. We have already met medical metaphor; the abrupt introduction of the anecdote can be paralleled in Horace, and no doubt has its origin in diatribe. Yet the very vigour and detail of Persius's picture tempt the reader to forget the drift:

> sed tremor inter vina subit calidumque trientem
> excutit e manibus, dentes crepuere retecti,
> uncta cadunt laxis tunc pulmentaria labris.
> hinc tuba, candelae, tandemque beatulus alto
> compositus lecto crassisque lutatus amomis
> in portam rigidas calces extendit. at illum
> hesterni capite induto subiere Quirites. (3.100 ff)

As he drinks his wine a fit of shaking comes over him, and knocks the hot glass from his hands: his bared teeth chatter, and greasy savouries tumble from his loosened lips. The upshot is trumpet and candles, and in due course the late lamented is laid out on a tall bier, and smeared with greasy spices he sticks out his stiff heels to the door. The pall-bearers wear caps on their heads, for yesterday they became Roman citizens.

The crude and cynical realism is worthy of Juvenal, who must have had this passage in mind when he described 'death after peacock' in his first satire. As well as being a poet in his own right, Persius deserves a little of the credit for Juvenal's success.

At last comes the application of the parable, which is sometimes misunderstood.

> tange, miser, venas et pone in pectore dextram—
> 'nil calet hic'—summosque pedes attinge manusque—
> 'non frigent': visa est si forte pecunia, sive
> candida vicini subrisit molle puella,
> cor tibi rite salit? (3.107 ff)

Feel your pulse, miserable man, and place your right hand on your breast. 'No temperature here.' Touch the extremities of your hands and feet. 'They aren't cold.' But suppose some money comes into view or you get a soft smile from the pretty girl next door, is your heart-beat steady then?

Persius addresses the 'patient' (who is really his lower self), and tells him to feel his pulse. *miser* shows that the moral invalid is being spoken to; one cannot agree with those editors who think that the patient is being insolent to the doctor. The patient thinks that there is nothing the matter with him (just like the man in the parable who disregarded medical advice). As far as physical illness is concerned, no doubt he is right, but he may still be suffering from spiritual infirmities.

And so to the conclusion:

> alges cum excussit membris timor albus aristas;
> nunc face supposita fervescit sanguis et ira
> scintillant oculi, dicisque facisque quod ipse
> non sani esse hominis non sanus iuret Orestes. (3.115 ff)

When white fear sticks up the bristles on your body, you are cold enough then all right. At other times your blood begins to boil as though you had been lit by a flame, your eyes spark with anger, and you say and do things which would seem indubitably mad even to mad Orestes.

This concluding passage is not well integrated with the previous section or with the rest of the satire; but the reader is perhaps reconciled by now to some structural incoherence. The mention of Orestes in the last line is meant to give a satiric colouring; he is one of the stock figures who came to Roman satire from Hellenistic philosophizing. As for the poem as a whole, one may feel that in spite of its lack of proportion (in more ways than one) it makes up for this by the vividness of its pictures and the virtuosity of its language. It might even be thought the best of the collection.

On the other hand, the fourth satire is both short and slight. It begins with a homily from the sage Socrates to the accomplished young politician Alcibiades.

> 'rem populi tractas?' (barbatum haec crede magistrum
> dicere, sorbitio tollit quem dira cicutae)
> 'quo fretus? dic hoc, magni pupille Pericli.
> scilicet ingenium et rerum prudentia velox
> ante pilos venit, dicenda tacendaque calles.
> ergo ubi commota fervet plebecula bile,
> fert animus calidae fecisse silentia turbae
> maiestate manus. quid deinde loquere? "Quirites,
> hoc puta non iustum est, illud male, rectius illud."' (4.1 ff)

'So you're handling the nation's business? (imagine the bearded teacher is speaking who was killed off by a fell gulp of hemlock). By what entitlement? Answer me that, ward of mighty Pericles. Your quick wits and early-won expertise have outgrown your moustache; you have a flair for when to speak and when to give no comment. And so when public opinion is inflamed and tempers are seething, your spirit moves you to still the multitude's passions with a majestic gesture. So far, so good; but what have you got to say? "Gentlemen, course A is wrong, B is no use, a better idea is C."'

This opening scene is admirable for its subtle blend of magniloquence and satire, and though it contains its quota of allusions it never becomes contorted or obscure. The first words refer to Plato's *Symposium*, where Alcibiades admits that he runs the country and neglects himself. *sorbitio* is not a grand word, and its conjunction with *dira* is a clever surprise. *quo fretus?* comes from the *First Alcibiades*, a dialogue rightly or wrongly attributed to Plato. The joke about the moustache is found in a Greek proverb and may have been a commonplace of diatribe. *fert animus* and *fecisse silentia* have a ring of high poetry, and *maiestate manus* is a fine coinage of Persius's own. *Quirites* gives a solemn touch, but the next line is phrased colloquially.

Socrates continues in more solemn vein. Alcibiades has studied philosophy, and ought to know something about right and wrong.

Why then does he not stop waving his tail (*caudam iactare*) at the flattery of the mob? The only aim of this handsome young politician is to have a good time for himself.

> 'exspecta, haut aliud respondeat haec anus. i nunc,
> "Dinomaches ego sum" suffla, "sum candidus". esto
> dum ne deterius sapiat pannucia Baucis,
> cum bene discincto cantaverit ocima vernae.' (4.19 ff)

'If you ask her this old hag would say just the same. Go on, spout away: "I'm an Alcmaeonid, and amn't I beautiful?" If you like, but you're no more a philosopher than a wizened peasant-woman peddling aphrodisiacs to dissolute slaves.'

That is to say, for purely selfish reasons the democratic politician sells harmful wares to unprincipled customers.

This opening passage is all very clever, but it lacks the greatest merit of satire: it has nothing to do with contemporary life. Plato had made some valid criticisms of Greek democracy, where an irresponsible assembly was led by inexpert politicians, but he was quite unrealistic about the actual virtues of a statesman. Persius makes matters worse by giving his sermon a local background: Alcibiades calls the people 'Quirites', the formal mode of addressing the Roman citizen-body. But the Roman assemblies had never had much direct influence over policy, and under the Empire none at all. Casaubon tried to save Persius's credit by making Alcibiades stand for Nero; in that case the smooth features of Seneca must be lurking behind Socrates's beard. But though some Stoics adopted a truculent attitude towards their rulers there is no reason to suppose that Persius would have tried anything so topical.

Persius goes on to complain that we are indifferent to our own faults: we only see the knapsack on the other man's back. Vettidius (an imaginary person) is so rich that a kite couldn't fly across his estates; so people think of him as a miser who grudges his slaves a good meal. Another man seems more relaxed, so nasty comments are made about his morals: here Persius allows himself some of the plain speaking traditional in Cynic diatribe and Roman satire. The drift of the argument is easily lost: Persius is not making a plea for tolerance in the Horatian manner, but simply observing that while we are indifferent to our own vices (the real point of the satire) we are ready enough to exaggerate our neighbour's faults. But the parenthetical portraits of the miser and the voluptuary are so detailed that the balance of the short satire is destroyed.

Finally Persius tries, not very successfully, to pull his poem together. If a man has hidden faults it is useless to disguise them or to protest that he enjoys the favour of the neighbourhood. If you really are a miser or a libertine there is no point in lending thirsty ears to the people's praises.

> respue quod non es; tollat sua munera cerdo.
> tecum habita: noris quam sit tibi curta supellex. (4.51 f)

Spit out what you are not; the shopkeeper can take his presents back. Live in your own house, and you will find out the inadequacy of your furniture.

But in spite of good sentences like these the satire as a whole fails to live up to its promise.

The fifth satire is the longest of the collection, and was regarded by Casaubon and Dryden, among others, as the best. It is better organized than the rest, and its tone is persistently elevated, but it ought by now to be recognized that this is not the most important of Persius's qualities. The satire begins with a hit at poets who ask for a hundred voices and a hundred tongues. Such pretentious openings are for writers in the grand style who deal with subjects like Thyestes's cook-pot (Thyestes in the play ate his children). Jokes at the expense of epic and tragedy are common in Roman satire from Lucilius to Juvenal. The serious poetry of the Silver Age was particularly irrelevant to any actual human activity, and Persius's criticisms were amply justified.

Persius claims that his own satires have more contact with the real world.

> verba togae sequeris iunctura callidus acri,
> ore teres modico, pallentis radere mores
> doctus et ingenuo culpam defigere ludo. (5.14 ff)

You imitate ordinary language, but your pungent juxtapositions are ingenious and your style, though not inflated, is well-rounded; you show your art by the way you scrape at vicious morals and nail a fault with well-bred banter.

Some of this is a fair analysis of Persius's own practice. He used

colloquialisms, but mixes them up with more serious elements.
As a creator of clever *iuncturae* (the placing together of two words
in an original and striking way) he has no rival except Horace.
teres suggests that he took trouble over his composition, yet he
avoids the *os rotundum* of the grand style. On the other hand, what
follows is less realistic. Lucilius had abused his enemies' vices
(though not out of high-mindedness), but Persius does not
attempt the mildest of criticisms. Persius also refers to Horace's
subtler methods; yet civilized teasing was as foreign to him as
abuse. He has described the subject-matter of Satire, not of his
own satires.

Persius now explains why he needs a hundred throats: he is
going to express his devotion to his revered teacher, the Stoic
Cornutus. Annaeus Cornutus may have been a freed man of the
Seneca family, though we are told that Persius was not captivated
by Seneca's own talents. He wrote on logic and rhetoric, and
Virgil's poetry; his one surviving work, an allegorical interpretation of Greek mythology, suggests that he was a bore. Yet he is
praised by Persius with all the unhealthy extravagance which
ancient sages exacted from their disciples:

> teneros tu suscipis annos
> Socratico, Cornute, sinu. tum fallere sollers
> adposita intortos extendit regula mores
> et premitur ratione animus vincique laborat
> artificemque tuo ducit sub pollice voltum. (5.36 ff)

You receive my young life, Cornutus, in your Socratic embrace. Then
with deceptive skill the rule is applied to twisted habits and straightens
them out; my mind is moulded by reason and struggles to be subdued,
and takes on features under your artist's thumb.

Fine words, but they fail to please. When the master was regarded
by the pupil with such uncritical veneration it is not surprising
that the schools stagnated. Persius even offers Cornutus an eloquent elaboration of the astrological fancies with which Horace
had cajoled Maecenas.

After his long introduction Persius now gets down to business.
He starts with a well-worn theme, the diversity of human aims.
One man is a merchant (this deserving class is treated unfairly by
ancient thinkers), another a glutton, another a gambler; but when
their joints grow old then they all realize that they have wasted

their lives. A fine passage follows on the dangers of procrastination. The theme was agreeable to moralists: St. Augustine, for instance, points out that 'cras, cras' is what the crow says.[18] Persius has nothing so striking as this touch, which would have appealed to him, but he handles the commonplace with distinction.

> 'cras hoc fiet idem'. cras fiat. 'quid? quasi magnum
> nempe diem donas?' sed cum lux altera venit,
> iam cras hesternum consumpsimus; ecce aliud cras
> egerit hos annos et semper paulum erit ultra. (5.66 ff)

'I can do it tomorrow just as well.' All right, do it tomorrow. 'What? D'you mean you regard a day as a big concession?' But when another sun shines, already we have used up yesterday's tomorrow; see, another tomorrow ladles the years away, and always keeps a little ahead.

cras hoc fiet idem belong together, as K. F. Hermann saw (compare Ovid, *Rem. Am.* 104 *dicimus assidue 'cras quoque fiet idem'*). The interpretation of *cras fiat* is due to Housman. No editor, so far as I know, has combined these two points; yet if either is rejected, the passage becomes very obscure.

Persius now comes to the main subject of his satire, the Stoic paradox that every fool is a slave and only the wise man free. Horace had handled the same theme in the seventh satire of his second book, but Persius's treatment has more of the true Stoic rigidity. He begins by describing the process of *manumissio per vindictam* and the symbolical twirling round by which a master could give a slave his liberty:

> heu steriles veri, quibus una Quiritem
> vertigo facit. hic Dama est non tresis agaso,[19]
> vappa lippus et in tenui farragine mendax.
> verterit hunc dominus, momento turbinis exit
> Marcus Dama. papae! Marco spondente recusas
> credere tu nummos? Marco sub iudice palles?
> Marcus dixit, ita est. adsigna, Marce, tabellas. (5.75 ff)

O men barren of the truth, for whom a single whirl can make a free citizen. Dama here is a twopenny stable-boy, a bleary tippler mendacious over a meagre feed. But let his master turn him round, in one short spin out he comes as Marcus Dama. I say! Marcus is surety, are you afraid to lend? Marcus is judge, do you turn white? Marcus has said so, it must be true. Could you witness my signature, Marcus?

After this promising start, Persius reverts to the mannerisms of his school. He imitates the close reasoning of the Stoic logicians.

'an quisquam est alius liber, nisi ducere vitam
cui licet ut libuit? licet ut volo vivere, non sum
liberior Bruto?' 'mendose colligis' inquit
Stoicus hic aurem mordaci lotus aceto,
'hoc relicum accipio, "licet" illud et "ut volo" tolle.' (5.83 ff)

'Nobody is free unless he is able to lead his life as he pleases. I am able to live as I want. Therefore I am more free than Brutus.' 'Your conclusion is false,' says the Stoic here, his ear rinsed with tingling vinegar. 'I accept your major premiss, but you must retract your "able" and "as I want".'

The metrical dialectic is pleasing, but not wholly original: Horace's butt, the Stoic Stertinius, had also talked in syllogisms (*Satires* 2.3.158 ff). Persius goes on to refer to the great jurist Masurius Sabinus; as Epictetus later did the same (4.3.12), one assumes that this is a Stoic commonplace. The dullness of the section is relieved by one magnificent line, *dum veteres avias tibi de pulmone revello* ('while I uproot the grannies from your chest'); but the lecture that follows is too earnest. 'Even if you lift a finger you do wrong' is one of the silliest of the Stoic paradoxes. 'The man at the mercy of his emotions is like a marionette pulled by strings': this is another Stoic cliché, used several times by Marcus Aurelius, though also found in Plato and in Horace (*Satires* 2.7.82).

There follow speeches by Avarice and Luxury. Such debates between abstracts were traditional in diatribe,[20] but this time Persius handles the motif with liveliness and wit.

mane piger stertis. 'surge' inquit Avaritia, 'eia,
surge'. negas. instat. 'surge' inquit. 'non queo.' 'surge.'
'et quid agam?' 'rogat! en saperdas advehe Ponto,
castoreum stuppas hebenum tus lubrica Coa;
tolle recens primus piper et sitiente camelo'. (5.132 ff)

Morning, and you're in bed snoring. 'Get up,' says Avarice, 'hi, get up.' You won't. She keeps on. 'Get up,' she says. 'Out of the question.' 'Get up.' 'What on earth for?' 'Listen to him. Import kippers from Russia, I tell you, along with castor, oakum, ebony, frankincense, oily Coan. Uplift this year's pepper before anybody else, and don't stop to give the camel a drink.'

It is interesting to compare Boileau's imitation:

> Le sommeil sur ses yeux commence à s'épancher:
> 'Debout', dit l'Avarice, 'il est temps de marcher.'
> —'Hé laissez-moi.'—'Debout.'—'Un moment.'—'Tu répliques?'
> —'A peine le Soleil fait ouvrir les boutiques.'
> —'N'importe, lève-toi.'—Pourquoi faire, après tout?'
> —'Pour courir l'Océan de l'un à l'autre bout,
> Chercher jusqu'au Japon la porcelaine et l'ambre,
> Rapporter de Goa le poivre et le gingembre.' (*Sat.* 8.69 ff)

Both passages are magnificent, but they are very different in style. Persius's dialogue is more vigorous, more amusing, and shorter: contrast *mane piger stertis* with the French version. His shopping-list has a ludicrous note which is absent from Boileau's resonant couplet. Boileau derives his theme from Persius, but in manner he is much closer to Horace's mature style.

Though Avarice makes her case so forcefully, Luxury sees some of the snags.

> 'tu mare transilias? tibi torta cannabe fulto
> cena sit in transtro Veientanumque rubellum
> exhalet vapida laesum pice sessilis obba?' (5.146 ff)

'*You* skim the seas? *You* dine on a thwart, with a coiled hawser for your cushion, while a squat noggin stinks Veientan rosso, spoilt by the flat resin?'

The passage is meant to be grotesque, but it would be wrong to regard it as obscure. An ancient reader would not have needed to look up *sessilis* and *obba,* and unlike some modern commentators he would have known about resinated wine. Luxury's positive policy is expressed more conventionally, but the clichés are made effective by the concentration of the writing.

> indulge genio, carpamus dulcia, nostrum est
> quod vivis, cinis et manes et fabula fies,
> vive memor leti, fugit hora, hoc quod loquor inde est. (5.151 ff)

Be nice to yourself, let's gather rosebuds, one life is all you get, soon you'll be dust and a ghost and a memory, remember it won't last, time flies, these words of mine diminish it.

The debate between Luxury and Avarice is successful because it contains lively phrases as well as improving sentiments.

Next comes a literary reminiscence from the *Eunuchus* of Menander. The adaptation is skilfully made, but it suffers from comparison with a similar passage in Horace (*Satires* 2.3.262 ff). What follows is more original:

> ius habet ille sui, palpo quem ducit hiantem
> cretata Ambitio? vigila et cicer ingere large
> rixanti populo, nostra ut Floralia possint
> aprici meminisse senes. (5.176 ff)

Is a man a free agent when he is petted and led along goggling by Lady Ambition, all clad in extra-white? Get up early and thrust beans lavishly on the squabbling populace, that our festival of Flora may be talked about by old men in the sunshine.

The noun *palpo* (from *palpare* 'to stroke') may be a happy coinage of Persius's own; Bücheler pointed out that it should be taken with *Ambitio* and not with *ille*. *cretata* is another vivid touch of satire: candidates at elections whitened their togas with chalk, which is why they were called *candidati*. The single word *aprici* summons up yet another picture. There follows an equally lively account of the superstitious man who observes Jewish or Egyptian rites; Persius anticipates Juvenal alike in the vigorous realism of his colouring and in his contempt for Oriental religions.

The satire ends with a rueful tailpiece, slightly self-mocking in the Horatian manner.

> dixeris haec inter varicosos centuriones,
> continuo crassum ridet Pulfenius ingens
> et centum Graecos curto centusse licetur. (5.189 ff)

Say this where the flat-footed sergeants can hear you, and at once hulking Pulfenius brays coarsely, and says a hundred Greeks aren't worth four and twopence.

Centurions get a bad press from the Roman satirists, no doubt deservedly. Horace has unhappy memories of his local school, which was dominated by the large sons of large centurions. Juvenal complains of their unfairness to the civilian (which suggests that he may never himself have been a high-ranking officer). But though Persius and Juvenal agree on centurions and Egyptians, they disagree on Greeks.

The sixth satire is addressed to Caesius Bassus, the only Latin

lyric poet, apart from Horace, whom Quintilian mentions by
name; after Persius's death he edited his poems for publication.

> admovit iam bruma foco te, Basse, Sabino?
> iamne lyra et tetrico vivunt tibi pectine chordae?
> mire opifex numeris veterum primordia vocum
> atque marem strepitum fidis intendisse Latinae,
> mox iuvenes agitare iocos et pollice honesto
> egregius lusisse senex. (6.1 ff)

Has winter now brought you, Bassus, to your Sabine fireside? Do the
lyre and the strings now come to life under your austere and truly
Sabine quill? You are a remarkable craftsman at setting to numbers
the beginnings of our ancient tongue and the virile hum of the Latin
harp; and even in your old age you know how to stir youthful frolics
and disport yourself with unimpeachable thumb.

Persius's manner is grander than usual, and also duller, but after
all he is talking to a real poet. In particular one may remark that
the first, fifth, and sixth lines have a caesura after the trochee in
the third foot: this metrical pattern is often found in the flowery
writings of the Silver Age, but the mannerism is alien to the
satirist's normal style. Such variation is less common in Persius
than in Horace and Juvenal, who often try fleeting imitations of
more pretentious writers.

Persius goes on to say that he is wintering at Luna, on the
Ligurian coast, near the modern La Spezia. This is one of his rare
personal allusions, but he cannot do for the beautiful Riviera di
Levante what Horace had done for his remote Sabine farm.

> mihi nunc Ligus ora
> intepet hibernatque meum mare qua latus ingens
> dant scopuli et multa litus se valle receptat.
> 'Lunai portum, est operae, cognoscite, cives.'
> cor iubet hoc Enni, postquam destertuit esse
> Maeonides Quintus pavone ex Pythagoreo. (6.6 ff)

For me the Ligurian coast is warm and my own sea is wintering where
the rocks present a huge cliff and the shore retreats in a deep gulf.
'Acquaint yourselves—it's worth your pains—with the port of Luna,
good people.' So bade the wise heart of Ennius, after he had desnored
the Maeonides of a Quintus, born from a Pythagorean peacock.

First Persius gives some poetical scene-painting, then a line from
the *Satires* of Ennius.[21] Finally he refers to the famous dream at

the beginning of the *Annals* in which Ennius learned that he had lived previously as Homer, and before that, as a peacock. *destertuit* is coined by Persius for the occasion, and given the construction of *destitit*; *Quintus* has caused confusion, but simply refers to Ennius's first name. After his pompous prelude the satirist has triumphantly resumed his normal idiom.

Persius goes on to profess indifference to the riches of his neighbours, and the Horatian reminiscences appropriately thicken:

> hic ego securus volgi et quid praeparet auster
> infelix pecori, securus et angulus ille
> vicini nostro quia pinguior, etsi adeo omnes
> ditescant orti peioribus, usque recusem
> curvus ob id minui senio aut cenare sine uncto
> et signum in vapida naso tetigisse lagoena. (6.12 ff)

Here I am indifferent to the crowd and the trouble that the south wind is brewing for the cattle, indifferent that the corner of my neighbour's land is more fertile than mine;—and even if all my inferiors grow rich, that's no reason why I should ever let myself droop with premature decay, or do without gravy to my dinner, or poke my nose into the seal on a flat bottle.

More satiric clichés follow: the twins with different temperaments, the miser seasoning his vegetables on his birthday, the ship-wrecked sailor exhibiting a picture of his shipwreck. These commonplaces are not a sign of unoriginality. The satiric genre developed late, and had less distinctive characteristics than the other literary categories. Satirists had to make it clear what they were writing, and it was a matter of pride to introduce the stock situations.

About half of the satire is taken up by an obscure and badly-arranged address to an imaginary heir. The fear of letting one's property go to a stranger was no doubt common in the Roman empire; many rich men were childless, and posthumous philan-thropy was less fashionable than in the Victorian age. But Persius's treatment has no relation to his own circumstances, and unlike Horace he fails to convince us that enlightened self-indulgence is a true facet of his character.

> 'tune bona incolumis minuas?' et Bestius urget
> doctores Graios: 'ita fit; postquam sapere urbi

> cum pipere et palmis venit nostrum hoc maris expers
> fenisecae crasso vitiarunt unguine pultes.' (6.37 ff)

'You're not going to impair your estate and get away with it'; and he harries the Greek teachers in the fashion of Bestius: 'The usual story; since this savourless taste of ours came to town with pepper and dates, the haymakers have spoiled their porridge with thick sauces.'

The passage is unusually cryptic, even for Persius. *maris expers* is borrowed from Horace (*Sat.* 2.8.15), where it refers to Chian wine; since some sorts of Chian wine were 'unmixed with sea-water' (Galen x, p. 833K) the phrase presumably means 'saltless' (not 'emasculate', as Casaubon and Housman took it). Commentators interpret *doctores* and *sapere* as 'philosophers' and 'philosophy', but it seems possible that 'gastronomes' and 'taste for food' are meant. Persius goes on to tell his unknown heir that he is going to celebrate a Roman victory. But not even here does he attempt a contemporary allusion: instead he has recourse to Caligula's ineffective German expedition, which took place when he was five.

Yet though Persius's theme is derivative and his argument confusing, he produces flashes of his old vivacity.

> age, si mihi nulla
> iam reliqua ex amitis, patruelis nulla, proneptis
> nulla manet patrui, sterilis matertera vixit
> deque avia nihilum superest, accedo Bovillas
> clivumque ad Virbi, praesto est mihi Manius heres. (6.52 ff)

Look here, if there's none left of my father's sisters or his brother's daughters, if my uncle's great-granddaughters are all gone and my maternal aunt has died without issue, and if no descendant of my grandmother survives, then off I go to Bovillae and up the hill of Virbius, and there I find waiting a beggar for my heir.

With a mixture of Stoic logic and Cynic cynicism he then shows that even Manius the beggar is some sort of relative; so his heir ought to be grateful that he is getting anything at all.

> qui prior es, cur me in decursu lampada poscis?
> sum tibi Mercurius; venio deus huc ego ut ille
> pingitur. an renuis? vis tu gaudere relictis? (6.61 ff)

You are running in front, so don't ask for the baton before I've finished the lap. I'm appearing to you like Mercury in the picture, but my money-bags are real. Do you mean you refuse them? You ought to be thankful for what's left.

Persius is not going to starve himself for the benefit of his heir's dissolute grandson:

> mihi trama figurae
> sit reliqua, ast illi tremat omento popa venter? (6.73 f)

Am I to be left with a thread of a figure while his priest-paunch wobble with fat?

And so to the brilliant conclusion of an uneven satire.

> vende animam lucro, mercare atque excute sollers
> omne latus mundi, ne sit praestantior alter
> Cappadocas rigida pinguis plausisse catasta.
> rem duplica, 'feci; iam triplex, iam mihi quarto,
> iam decies redit in rugam. depunge ubi sistam,
> inventus, Chrysippe, tui finitor acervi.' (6.75 ff)

Sell your soul for profit, be a true trader and shrewdly ransack every continent, so that you have no superior at smacking plump Cappadocians on the hard[22] auction-planks. Double your capital. 'I have already done so. Now threefold, now fourfold, now tenfold have I folded it. Pin-point a stopping-place, and you have found the solution to Chrysippus's *sorites*.'

Chrysippus was the third head of the Stoic school, and some of his logical theories are still regarded as important.[23] The most notorious of his problems was the so-called 'sorites': how many grains do you remove from a heap before it ceases to be a heap? The scholiast tells us that some lines were deleted by Persius's executors at the end of the book; if so, they did their work skilfully. To Horace, Chrysippus was a Greek who wrote a lot of dull books: to Persius he was a serious philosopher.

Persius is conventionally accused of unoriginality, but his idiom is individual and has not been imitated. He is called obscure, but a reader familiar with the abruptness of diatribe would have found him less disconcerting. In any case obscurity is not the greatest fault of poets: insipidity is worse, and Persius is never that. He is undeniably grotesque; but satire could permit, and the twentieth century should condone, a certain angularity. He is said to be humourless, but his brisk dialogues and bizarre metaphors refute the charge. He had only one style, and major poets have more; but it is not the thesis of this paper that he was a major poet. He draws less directly on life than could be wished, but there is more than one way of writing poetry, and his attitudes are serious, consistent, and authentic. Above all he can write, and it is the ability to write (more than anything else) that distinguishes poets from other men. If you, reader, can do as well when you are twenty-seven, you will deserve more than the clumsy misapprehensions and patronizing rebukes which have been the fate of Persius.

NOTES

1 The only reliable text is by W. V. Clausen; the edition of 1959 (with Juvenal) is sufficient for most purposes. There are valuable commentaries by Jahn (1843), Conington (1893), Villeneuve (1918). Translations are provided by Conington, and by G. G. Ramsay (Loeb, 1918).

2 'Persius also left to us onely one boke by the whiche he commyttyd his name and laude to perpetuall memory' (Alexander Barclay in the preface to his *Ship of Fools*, 1509).

3 For testimonia see the edition by Santi Consoli, Rome, 1911.

4 R. M. Alden, *The Rise of Formal Satire in England* (Philadelphia, 1899); J. Peter, *Complaint and Satire in Early English Literature* (Oxford, 1956).

5 *Essai sur Perse* (Paris, 1918).

6 *Classical Quarterly* 7 (1913), 12 ff.

7 E. Guilpin, *Skialetheia* (1598), epig. 70:

> I know thow'lt doome them to th'*Apotheta*
> To wrap Sope in, and *Assifoetida*.

8 *Post-Augustan Poetry* (Oxford, 1909).

9 Mr. G. J. Toomer convinced me that *tantae* is wrong; Mr. A. F. Wells suggested *tentae* in an impromptu discussion, before we knew of Barth's emendation.

10 Aulus Gellius 12.2.10 *duros quosdam versus et enormes*.

11 The *edictum* is surely the praetor's edict, and not, as some commentators suppose, a play-bill.

12 The future *apponet* is a variant here. But Persius means simply that a birthday marks the passing of the years; he is not predicting for his friend a long and happy life.

13 For this and the following instance see *Classical Quarterly* N.S. 9 (1959), 73 ff.

14 Some parallels are quoted by E. S. McCartney, *Classical Philology* 43 (1948), 184 ff (I owe this reference to Dr. S. Weinstock).

15 *Classical Philology* 23 (1928), 337 ff.

16 See also J. Tate, 'Was Persius a Micher?' (*Classical Review* 42 (1928), 62 ff.; cf. 43 (1929), 56 ff.)

17 Imitated inadequately by Hall, *Virgidemiarum* ii, 2.47 ff.

[18] *In Psalm* 102.16, *Serm.* 82.14, 224.4, Caes. Arel. *Serm.* 18.6, Cassiod. *Hist.*
5.27. I cannot resist quoting Barclay's *Ship of Fools*:

> They folowe the crowes cry to theyr great sorowe
> Cras cras cras to morowe we shall amende
> And if we mende nat then, than shall we the next morowe
> Outher shortly after, we shall no more offende
> Amende mad fole whan god this grace doth sende
> He is unwyse whiche trustes the crowes songe
> And that affermyth that he shall lyve so longe.

[19] cf. Skelton, *Garland of Laurel*, 'tressis agasonis species prior, altera Davi'.
[20] See Lejay's edition of Horace's *Satires*, p. lxv. His introduction illuminates
the connexion between diatribe and satire.
[21] Housman, *Classical Review* 48 (1934), 50 f.
[22] *rigida* is contrasted with *pinguis*. I cannot see why commentators interpret
it as 'high'.
[23] See W. Kneale and M. Kneale, *The Development of Logic* (Oxford, 1962).

SATIRE AND REALISM IN PETRONIUS

J. P. Sullivan

I. *The Literary and Social Background*

ALTHOUGH Petronius is regarded as one of the most 'modern' of ancient authors because of his very direct appeal to us, the brute critical fact is that the *Satyricon* is one of the strangest and most untypical works that have come down to us from classical antiquity. The seductive feeling of modernity, due partly to its resemblance to some contemporary novels, has been a stumbling-block to any literary discussion of the work. Such discussion has been generally confined to *Quellenforschung*, to a consideration of the models Petronius used for various episodes. Until this feeling of unclassical 'modernity' and this feeling of strangeness are resolved, the understanding requisite to correct evaluation is impossible. In what follows I shall try to suggest why the *Satyricon* is what it is and not any other thing, and how the work is as much as any other work a product of the circumstances of its age and its author, and how such an understanding allows us to comment on its merits and evaluate its originality.

The long dispute about the date and authorship of the *Satyricon* has made difficult a consideration of the historical circumstances in which the work came into existence, and yet for a work like the *Satyricon* the circumstances of its composition and the audience at which it was aimed are of paramount importance. It does not belong to a recognized genre like epic, a genre in which the most bookish and antiquarian of authors could work without any large consideration of modernity or sophisticated taste—the mere existence of Homer, Ennius, and Virgil is explanation enough of Valerius Flaccus, Silius Italicus and Nonnus. The *Satyricon*, however, cannot be explained without some reference to its immediate circumstances. Now, I am quite convinced that the *Satyricon* is a product of the Neronian age;[1] I am also reasonably certain that it was written by the Petronius who was Nero's Arbiter of Elegance and whose death is described by Tacitus in *Annals* 16.18–19 as follows:[2]

Petronius deserves some further attention. He was a man who spent his days sleeping and his nights working or enjoying himself. Industry is the usual foundation of success, but with him it was idleness. Unlike most people who throw away their money in dissipation, he was not regarded as an extravagant sensualist, but as one who made luxury a fine art. His conversation and his way of life were unconventional with a certain air of nonchalance, and they charmed people all the more by seeming so unstudied. Yet as proconsul in Bithynia and later as consul, he showed himself a vigorous and capable administrator. His subsequent return to his old habits, whether this was real or apparent, led to his admission to the small circle of Nero's intimates, where he became the Arbiter of Elegance. In the end Nero's jaded appetite regarded nothing as enjoyable or refined unless Petronius had given his sanction to it. Consequently the jealousy of Tigellinus was aroused against him: he saw in Petronius a rival, someone superior to himself in the whole art of pleasure. So he worked upon the Emperor's cruelty, that master-passion to which all his other lusts gave way. Accusing Petronius of being an intimate of Scaevinus, he bribed a slave to give evidence against him. Petronius did not have a chance to reply and Tigellinus flung the best part of his household into prison.

The Emperor at that time happened to be on a visit to Campania. Petronius got as far as Cumae and was prevented from going any farther. He refused to prolong the suspense that hope or fear involved. Not that he was hasty in taking leave of life. On the contrary, he opened his veins and then, as the fancy took him, he bound them up or re-opened them. Meanwhile he talked to his friends, but not on serious topics or anything calculated to win admiration for his stoicism. He listened to their contributions—not discussions about the immortality of the soul or the views of philosophers, but simply gay songs and light verse. He dealt out rewards to some of his slaves and floggings to others. He had a good dinner served and slept for a while, so that his death, although forced on him, should appear natural. Even in the codicils to his will, he refused to put down any of the usual death-bed flatteries for Nero or Tigellinus or any of the other courtiers. Instead he wrote out a full description of the Emperor's vicious activities, prefaced with the names of his male and female partners, and specifying

74

the novel forms his lust had taken. This document he sent under seal to Nero. Then he broke his signet ring in case it should be used later to endanger others.

Nero's puzzlement as to how his nocturnal ingenuities were known was resolved by blaming Silia. This was a not insignificant person, a senator's wife in fact, who had been a chosen partner in all the Emperor's vices and also a close friend of Petronius. She was exiled for her lack of discretion about what she had seen and experienced.

If we combine the evidence of the work itself, the evidence furnished us by Tacitus in the above passage and what we know from such authors as Persius and Seneca about the historical and literary ambience of the age, it seems clear that the *Satyricon* was almost certainly a work written for Nero's sophisticated and highly literary court circle. Whatever Nero's moral failings, he was an Emperor who was more interested in literature than any Emperor since Augustus, and his motives, being the personal motives of an interested practitioner, were perhaps purer than those of that great propagandist. Tacitus does not mention Petronius' writings any more than he mentions Seneca's, but it is in the last degree unlikely that Petronius' functions as Arbiter of Elegance at the court were confined to the choice of the proper spoons for woodpecker *en cocotte* or to the acquisition of myrrhine wine-dippers, and we know from the above passage that he did not play the part of master of the revels in Nero's less literary debaucheries.

If the *Satyricon* then is a work directed primarily to a coterie, this will explain not only the neglect of the work in the succeeding centuries (for such works, however brilliant they be, stand less chance of attention from the general reader than those written with an eye upon the great literary world and posthumous fame), but also the choice of literary form. As Arbiter of Elegance in a literary circle, Petronius would obviously take on the function of critic, as well as the role of an experimental artist. The vehicles of ancient literary criticism were, of course, satires such as Horace *Sat.* 1.4 and Persius *Sat.* 1, epistles such as Horace's Epistle to the Pisos, or the more technical treatise. For recitation to a circle the epistle is surely too artificial a genre, and as Petronius' critical techniques include parody and imitation, clearly the treatise form is equally unsuitable, even if we disregard the fact that Petronius was himself a practising poet[3] and prose writer. The choice of satire, even apart from other considerations, was almost inevitable, and as his criticisms were to include criticism of contemporary oratory and prose writing, Menippean satire, a well-developed literary form in Roman literature, becomes an equally obvious choice. The *Ludus de morte Claudii* indicates that it was a current form and so available for use and development without any resuscitation.

This choice of literary genre explains in turn other features of the work. Satire is a flexible form in Roman literature and handles subjects such as a Journey to Brundisium which our own narrower definition of satire would not describe as satire at all. None the less there were many topics used by the satirists from Lucilius on which do conform with our definition and it is from these that our own definition has evolved. Such traditional themes would therefore force themselves on Petronius. However original a Roman writer might be, he was still more conscious of tradition, of the appropriate subjects and their treatment in each literary genre, than any modern: nor could the expectations of one's audience be disregarded in the adoption of a given form. Petronius moreover, is not as revolutionary in some ways as, say, Lucan. Petronius' touchstones were the usual ones: Homer, Demosthenes, Cicero, Vergil and Horace (cf. 5, 118) and his reactions to Lucan's innovations in the epic are patently unfavourable (118). As a result, the rehandling of familiar satirical themes in his episodic work occasions no surprise: hence Trimalchio's dinner party, which owes much to Horace's description of the dinner of Nasidienus (*Sat.* 2.8), the satire on legacy-hunting and on high-class ladies such as Circe, who preferred slaves as lovers, a subject familiar to us from Herondas.

It will become obvious, however, that Petronius' use of specifically satirical themes did not go hand in hand with the adoption of a coherent moral standpoint from which genuine satirists criticize vice, folly or other aberrations by reference to some sort of positive standards. Petronius substitutes for this something much more specialized and it is this fact that leads into the core of the work. But before saying anything of this central problem, there is more explanation to be offered of the elements that make up the work.

So far we have seen how the decision to write literary criticism, parody and poetic exercises determined Petronius' choice of form and how in turn this determined partially the selection of satiric themes which could provide episodes for the loose picaresque plot. Now satire with its tradition of *sermoni propriora* (in Horace's phrase) and its set of traditional subjects represents one of the strains of realism in Roman literature: *quidquid agunt homines, hominem pagina nostra sapit, quodque facit populus, candida lingua refert*—all of these phrases summarize its subject-matter and attitude. At least one association of satire was with the seamier side of life, the low sexual elements which were kept out of the more elevated literary forms. The mere choice of the satiric form, however, does not explain fully the presence in Petronius of so much sexual material that Adrianus Turnebus could say 'Petronius Arbiter venustatem orationis suae inquinavit spurcissimis amoribus.' It explains only the *acceptability* of such material on literary grounds. Even satire had developed from its rude stylistic beginnings, according to Horace (*Sat.* 1.10, 64 ff), and a further explanation is needed of the extensive use by the Arbiter of Elegance of gross sexual themes, often of a perverted nature, which are deployed humorously but not satirically.

To understand this juxtaposition of the gross and the highly sophisticated in Petronius we must look more closely at the conditions of the age and the audience. Historians such as Tacitus and Suetonius offer us a vivid and scarifying picture of Neronian society. For all its material luxury and literary sophistication it was a society which another age would unhesitatingly classify as decadent and depraved. Societies which combine a high degree of sophistication and indeed civilization with immorality and decadence are common enough: one thinks of the Gay Nineties in England and its continental equivalents. J. K. Huysman's *A rebours* and Oscar Wilde's *The Picture of Dorian Gray* are typical products of that era.[4] In both of these, amid all the exotic culture we find clearly delineated a certain *nostalgie de la boue*, which seems to have been a characteristic of Nero's circle also. Quite apart from the sexual excesses described by Tacitus and Suetonius, we know from the latter (*Nero* 26) that the Emperor liked to wander in the more disreputable parts of Rome and play the mohock with respectable Roman citizens. Given the society, this is not psychologically surprising and this interest is mirrored in the *Satyricon* not only by the realistic portrayal of a highly vulgar milieu at Puteoli[5] but also in the many episodes involving Quartilla,

Eumolpus, Circe, the children of Philomela, and the original trio, Encolpius, Ascyltus, and Giton. These sections would all titillate the tastes of the circle, much as gossip about the sexual activities of the Emperor was interesting to Petronius (Tac. *Ann.* 16.19).

II. *A Digression on the Genesis of the Sexual Episodes*[6]

THE literary and social determinants of the sexual episodes do not take us the whole way; a further explanation may be offered of the *type* of material used.[6] Some aspects need little discussion. The assumption of bisexuality is part of Roman thinking on such matters and is an assumption shared by Catullus, Tibullus, Juvenal, and Martial, to name but a few. Again, some of Petronius' material seems literary, the story of the Widow of Ephesus is a *prima facie* example. (It will not do, however, to stress a literary provenience too much when offering genetic explanations: the very *choice* of material from earlier authors may be significant: in the case of Petronius the impotence theme (128 ff), familiar to us from Ovid's treatment of the same subject in *Amores* 3.7, is susceptible of further analysis.) The most striking feature, however, of the sexual material in Petronius is that it fits a certain pattern of psychosexuality, a pattern of such a striking sort that it deserves closer attention.

It is a reasonable assumption that an author's choice of sexual themes will reflect more than most choices of material his conscious or unconscious preoccupations. The pattern of the sexual episodes in Petronius, as it happens, is a markedly individual one not found in the rest of ancient literature. Petronius is the first author I know of whose interests, as shown in his work, are predominantly voyeuristic. Other references to this orientation in ancient literature are very rare.[7] The primary evidence in Petronius is clear: Quartilla and Encolpius watch the love-play of Pannychis and Giton through a hole in the door (26), and an almost identical incident occurs in 140, where a little boy with Encolpius spies on Eumolpus and Philomela's little nymphet. Considering the starkly repetitious nature of these two episodes of *scopomixia*, both involving scenes of a perverse nature, even by ancient standards (cf. Encolpius' comment at 25.3), this is evidence enough for Petronius' interests. For those, however, who are sympathetic towards evidence based on psychoanalytic theory a great deal more may be said which brings almost the whole of the sexual material in the *Satyricon* into one clear pattern based on the psycho-sexual polarities of scopophilia.

The transformations of scopophilia are as important as its obvious manifestation and in the *Satyricon* examples of its direct psychoanalytical polarity, exhibitionism, are even more frequent and almost as obvious. Episodes which exemplify this trait in one way or another are to be found (in diminishing order of obviousness) in 24 (Quartilla's examination of Giton), 140 (Encolpius' exhibiting himself to Eumolpus), 105 (where Lichas recognizes Encolpius from his genitals), 11 (where Ascyltus interrupts the lovemaking of Encolpius and Giton), and 92 (Ascyltus at the baths—which may be construed as exhibitionism or voyeurism indifferently). Nor is this all. To see how pervasive a theme scopophilia is in the *Satyricon*, it is only necessary to examine the episodes in the light of Freud's scheme of the varied aspects of the instinct which is as follows:[8]

α Subject's looking at his own sexual organ	= Subject's own sexual organ being looked at by himself
β Subject's looking at an *extraneous object* (active scopophilia)	γ Subject's own sexual organ being looked at by another person (exhibitionism)

(It is incidentally irrelevant whether the fictional characters expose themselves of their own accord or through circumstances, for the author's fantasy is autonomous here.)

The incidents in the *Satyricon* of active scopophilia and of exhibitionism (Freud's types β and γ) have been described, but there are also obvious instances of Freud's α category. In 140 Encolpius finds himself impotent and later, when alone, he attempts to castrate himself: frustrated in this he then abuses his inadequate member for failing him. Such an incident plainly falls into Freud's α category: even the dual nature of that category is realized, as Encolpius and his penis are treated as separate objects occupying our attention in turn. The very ambivalence of Encolpius in this castration attempt (is his penis part of himself or not?) suggests the auto-erotism underlying scopophilia. Petronius, in fact, illustrates all the Freudian classifications, not aetiologically as Freud does, but as different aspects of the same preoccupation.

If all this is granted, certain other choices of incident may be related to the less obvious transformations of this instinct. Obscene humour and wit represent exposure in a psychological sense and the frequent examples of obscene wit in the conversations are perhaps not irrelevant (e.g. *Tanto magis expedit inguina quam ingenia fricare*—92). But more important, scopophilia particularly shows itself in the desire to see what is forbidden, whether by law, social custom or, ultimately, incest taboos. Two quotations are apposite here:

'Knowing sexual facts' may substitute for the observation of sexual facts and become a sexual aim of its own . . .[9]

And Abraham's remarks on a neurotic patient:

. . . the early forcing away of his scopophilic instinct from its real objects and aims led not only to a typical brooding but also to a morbid propensity towards secret and mystical things . . . I need hardly refer to the countless similar phenomena that are to be found in folk-psychology—on the one hand, secret cults, mysteries, occultist movements, etc., and on the other, religious prohibitions against enquiring into the most secret things.[10]

Now the emphasis on *secrets* in one episode in the *Satyricon* must strike even the most casual reader: the word *secretum* occurs frequently. The offence which ran the trio foul of Quartilla was the witnessing and consequent profanation of the rites of Priapus (16.3, 17.9). Quartilla stresses the secret nature of these rites (*tot annorum secreta*) and the danger of their becoming common knowledge. Throughout the episode there are allusions to these secrets (cf. 21 *passim*). There is even a retelling in the Petronian fragments of the story of Midas and his ears with the moral that men cannot keep secrets (*Nam citius flammas mortales ore tenebunt quam secreta tegant*—fr. 28).

Almost all of the sexual themes can be subsumed under this scopophilic pattern if we consider the vicissitudes of this impulse as discovered in psychoanalytic theory and practice. The motif of castration, for example, occurs in two episodes. The first is Giton's move to castrate himself with a blunted razor because his sexual attractions have caused so much jealousy among his friends (108.10); the second is Encolpius' frustrated attempt to castrate himself because of his sexual inadequacy with Circe (132.8). Now castration anxiety may be understood as the fear of punishment for forbidden looking, and this may be related to the various references to the Cyclops story, which is alluded to several times in the *Satyricon* (48, 97, 98, 101) and which clearly fascinated Petronius. One instance of this is psychoanalytically interesting. Trimalchio, displaying his inaccurate knowledge of mythology, asks Agamemnon at one point (48) if he knows the story of Ulysses, how the Cyclops tore his thumb off with pincers (*numquid . . . tenes . . . de Ulixe fabulam, quemadmodum illi Cyclops pollicem poricino extorsit?*). Here the underlying notion of castrating the father seems to have been replaced by the more basic anxiety that the father will castrate oneself. Trimalchio's freudian slip is therefore of considerable interest.

Inasmuch as Encolpius' attempt at self-castration takes place after his sexual failure with Circe, this connects the motif with the recurrent theme of sexual inadequacy and sexual envy. Abraham mentions a patient, a scopophilic, who had once seen his father naked when he was nine years old and

. . . had inspected his genitals with great interest. His phantasies . . . reverted to that scene. And yet the thoughts associated with it were by no means purely pleasurable; on the contrary, he was continually worried by the question whether his genitals would attain the size of his father's . . . he fell prey to the tormenting belief . . . that his penis was too small.[11]

Two situations in the *Satyricon* are reminiscent of this: the jealous reference to the size of Ascyltus' genitals (92), Ascyltus, of course, being a rival for Giton's affections, and the final return to normal of Encolpius' own genitals (139), when he exhibits them to his other rival, Eumolpus, a fatherly figure (83.7, 98.8, 100.5) with strong sexual inclinations (94.5). Feelings of sexual inferiority is often a motive for certain types of scopophilia, particularly for male interest in male genitals. It is to be noticed that Encolpius, the narrator and hero (or anti-hero), is the one who principally exemplifies the pattern: it is he who displays sexual inadequacy, sexual envy (92.12), castration anxiety, and scopophilic and exhibitionist traits to the full; he seems therefore the main vehicle of the author's phantasy in these respects, just as Eumolpus is the main vehicle of the author's views on poetry. Encolpius, of course, is not made out to be a sympathetic character, but more of a psychological scapegoat.

One final aspect of scopophilia may be mentioned: its connexion with sadistic impulses.[12] It must be obvious to the most casual reader that many of the sexual scenes in the *Satyricon* are sadistic in their implications. Encolpius' jealous protest that the seven-year-old Pannychis is too young for the burdens she is called upon to bear is followed by his scopophilic participation in her defloration. The situation is not so very different when the young daughter of Philomela is seduced by the lecherous Eumolpus (140), although here no scruples are expressed by Encolpius. The scene where Ascyltus interrupts Encolpius and Giton in their love-making (11) and Ascyltus thrashes Encolpius soundly (*non perfunctorie*) is surely of a sadistic nature. This possibility seems more or less confirmed by the incident in which Encolpius takes great delight in watching through a hole in the door (!) the savage attack on Eumolpus (96.1). The other sadistic scenes which may be adduced to confirm this perhaps strange thesis are the ignominious expulsion of the impotent Encolpius (132.2, 3) and the attempts of Oenothea to arouse Encolpius' deficient virility (138).[12]

III. *The Realism of Petronius*

What has been said about *nostalgie de la boue* and the general and specific choice of sexual themes does not end the matter, although it may do something to remove the feeling of strangeness with which one initially faces the *Satyricon*. There is also a literary choice backed by literary principles which determines the direction of work, that is to say, there is something more than a willingness to gratify certain expectations in a coterie or an indulgence in sexual fantasy. Petronius' decision to write in certain way springs also from his literary views.

The literary criticism in the *Satyricon* represents Petronius' own views, even though it is expressed by such disreputable characters as the narrator, Agamemnon or Eumolpus, and thus offers further insight into the principles of the work. It may, of course, be objected that the author in giving his criticism such dubious expression is disclaiming responsibility for, perhaps even parodying, these literary opinions. Nevertheless the consistency of these views, unexpected from such divergent sources if we are looking for parody, and the fact that we have none but disreputable sources anyway for the serious criticism which we have postulated as part of Petronius' purpose in writing the work, blunts this objection—after all, there is general agreement that the famous defence of the work at 132 is to be taken seriously, even though it is put into Encolpius' mouth in a particularly ridiculous context.

Petronius' literary position is this: he disliked contemporary rhetoric and rhetorical training. Consider the opening passage:

'num alio genere furiarum declamatores inquietantur, qui clamant: "haec vulnera pro libertate publica excepi, hunc oculum pro vobis impendi; date mihi [ducem] qui me ducat ad liberos meos, nam succisi poplites membra non sustinent"? haec ipsa tolerabilia essent, si ad eloquentiam ituris viam facerent. nunc et rerum tumore et sententiarum vanissimo strepitu hoc tantum proficiunt, ut cum in forum venerint, putent se in alium orbem terrarum delatos. et ideo ego adulescentulos existimo in scholis stultissimos fieri, quia nihil ex his quae in usu habemus aut audiunt aut vident, sed piratas cum catenis in litore stantes, sed tyrannos edicta scribentes quibus imperent filiis ut patrum suorum capita praecidant, sed responsa in pestilentiam data ut virgines tres aut plures immolentur, sed mellitos verborum globulos et omnia dicta factaque quasi papavere et sesamo sparsa. qui inter haec nutriuntur non magis sapere possunt quam bene olere qui in culina habitant. pace vestra liceat dixisse, primi omnium eloquentiam perdidistis. levibus enim atque inanibus sonis ludibria quaedam excitando effecistis ut corpus orationis enervaretur et caderet. nondum iuvenes declamationibus continebantur, cum Sophocles aut Euripides invenerunt verba quibus deberent loqui. nondum umbraticus doctor ingenia deleverat, cum Pindarus novemque lyrici Homericis versibus canere timuerunt. et ne poetas [quidem] ad testimonium citem, certe neque Platona neque Demosthenen ad hoc genus exercitationis accessisse video. grandis et ut ita dicam pudica oratio non est maculosa nec turgida, sed naturali pulchritudine exsurgit. nuper ventosa istaec et enormis loquacitas Athenas ex Asia commigravit animosque iuvenum ad magna surgentes veluti pestilenti quodam sidere afflavit, semelque corrupta regula eloquentia stetit et obmutuit. quis postea ad summam Thucydidis, quis Hyperidis ad famam processit? ac ne carmen quidem sani coloris enituit, sed omnia quasi eodem cibo pasta non potuerunt usque ad senectutem canescere. Pictura quoque non alium exitum fecit, postquam Aegyptiorum audacia tam magnae artis compendiarium invenit.'

'Our professional speakers are hag-ridden in the same way, surely, when they shout, "*I got these wounds fighting for freedom! I lost this eye for you. Give me a hand to lead me to my children. I'm hamstrung, my legs can't support me.*" We could put up with even this stuff if it were a royal road to eloquence. But the only result of this pomposity, this empty thunder of platitudes, is that when young speakers first enter public life they think they've been landed on another planet. I'm sure the reason such young nitwits are produced in our schools is that they've no contact with anything of any use in everyday life. All they get is pirates standing on the beach dangling manacles, dictators writing orders for sons to cut off their fathers' heads, oracles advising the sacrifice of three virgins or so during a plague—a mass of sickly sentiments: every word, every move just so much poppycock!

'People fed on this kind of thing have as much chance of learning sense as dishwashers have of smelling clean. If you'll pardon my saying so, you professors of rhetoric are mainly responsible. You have ruined good speaking. Your silly noises became some sort of amusement and as a result you took the guts out of real oratory. And that was the end of it. Young men were not tied down to rhetorical exercises when Sophocles and Euripides managed to write the way people should speak. Academic pedants had not addled their wits when Pindar and the nine lyric poets grew nervous of the Homeric style. And apart from the poets I can cite, I certainly cannot see Plato or Demosthenes going in for this sort of thing. The elevated, what one might call the *pure* style, is not full of purple patches and bombast: it is lifted up by its intrinsic beauty. It is not so long since that long-winded spouting of yours travelled from Asia to Athens and its foul pestilential breath infected every youthful ambition. Once standards drop, eloquence loses vigour and voice. Who since then has attained the stature of Thucydides or the reputation of Hyperides? Why, not even poetry has shown a spark of life. All forms of literature have been faced with the same diet and lost their chance of a ripe old age. Even the great art of painting has met the same fate since the unscrupulous Egyptians produced their Handbook for Painters.'

Agamemnon then defends the traditional literary education which is a prerequisite to good oratory (5); here the influence of oratory on even non-oratorical prose should not be forgotten. Agamemnon's exhortations are very similar in outlook to the recommendations Eumolpus offers the would-be epic poet (118), a long soaking in the great writers: one has to be well-read (*plenus litteris*). Another similarity between the discussions of oratory and of epic poetry is the reaction in both to the purple passage, the noise-mongering, the unintegrated pieces of fine writing whether in the form of epigrams or bombast. *Grandis et ut ita dicam pudica oratio non est maculosa nec turgida*, says Encolpius; and Eumolpus strikes the same chord when he speaks of the *controversiam sententiolis vibrantibus pictam* and warns that in poetry care must be taken that the epigrams do not stand out from the texture of the poem—*curandum est ne sententiae emineant extra corpus orationis expressae* (118.5).

This view of the consistency and genuineness of the literary views in the *Satyricon* is supported by the fact that the very style of Petronius, the lucid, simple language which might be described as a form of *sermo urbanus* (it is after all the narrative medium), may be regarded as a reaction to contemporary writing. It is as different as possible from the writing of another major literary figure of Neronian times, Seneca. There is no need to postulate any perverse or political reaction to Senecan literary ideals in Petronius: the tradition of a sort of Attic simplicity was a good one in Roman literary theory and the *simplicitas* Tacitus observed in Petronius' character might well be paralleled by a literary *simplicitas* based on genuinely held critical principles. These principles in prose fit well with his views on poetry. The objection, patently directed at Lucan, to the epigrammatic style of poetry and the adduction of Augustan touchstones such as Vergil and Horace are of a piece with these principles.

These threads come together in the well-known *credo* put in the mouth of Encolpius, a *credo* which serves simultaneously as a defence of Petronius' subjects and his treatment. The passage deserves quotation in full:

> quid me constricta spectatis fronte Catones
>   damnatisque novae simplicitatis opus?
> sermonis puri non tristis gratia ridet,
>   quodque facit populus, candida lingua refert.
> nam quis concubitus, Veneris quis gaudia nescit?
>   quis vetat in tepido membra calere toro?
> ipse pater veri doctos Epicurus amare
>   iussit et hoc vitam dixit habere τέλος. (132)

Why do you look at me with a frown, you Catos, and condemn my work of fresh simplicity? The happy charm of a pure style smiles in its pages and my candid tongue relates what ordinary folk do. After all, who is unaware of sex and the pleasures of Love? Who is against bodies kindling in a warm bed? The father of truth himself, Epicurus, bade philosophers love and he said this was life's *summum bonum*.

The stylistic claims here are not all. The main object of the poem is, of course, to vindicate on general grounds Petronius' choice of bawdy subject-matter: it represents *reality*—what everyone does—and it is ethically in accord with Epicurean doctrines as generally interpreted at this period. But the manifesto also fits in with the criticism of the unreality of oratorical themes in the schools, not to mention some of the contemporary prose literature of the period such as Seneca's Letters to Lucilius.[13] Indeed, if the *Satyricon* is not a direct attack on Senecan writing, it is surely an attack on the sort of thing Seneca wrote in the Letters to Lucilius. Tacitus' description of how Petronius spent his last hours is worth referring to.

The explanation of purpose then covers much more than the sexual themes. *Quodque facit populus, candida lingua refert* might well be the epigraph of the *Cena Trimalchionis*, which is generally acknowledged as the example *par excellence* of realistic description in the work, notably in the meticulous detail of the vulgar dialogue, the description of the dinner, the careful depiction of Trimalchio's character and his habitat, and the impression of verisimilitude which the use of a naïve commentator gives.

The realism of the *Cena* is our main concern here and a discussion of its satirical bases may be postponed for the moment. The artistry of the episode, which is far removed from the realism of the sprawling modern documentary novel, must not be underrated. There is no attempt at a phonographic or photographic realism. To begin with, the structure of the *Cena* is based on such literary models as Horace's *Cena Nasidieni* and, perhaps indirectly, on Plato's *Symposium*; the studied rhythmical progression through the successive acts is deliberatively contrived with such well-planned digressions as the ghost stories of 61–63. The portrait of Trimalchio is built up, first indirectly, by a description of his physical circumstances, then through the eyes of an admiring friend, and only later does he begin revealing himself through his behaviour, conversation and autobiography. It is the careful detail of the incidents, the elaborate impressionistic pastiche of vulgar speech and lower-class platitudinizing in the mouths of Trimalchio and his guests that provide the feeling of authenticity.[14]

This artistic realism goes hand in hand with the pointed exaggeration which gives this section of the work its claim to be a humorous masterpiece. The humour, like the realism, is prompted to some extent by a satirical motive; but humour is not necessarily at odds with realism, even though nowadays the latter is mainly associated with the serious sociological novel such as James Farrell's *Studs Lonigan* and other detailed documentary novels. Humour frequently operates in a setting of realism; as one writer has put it, 'The added element is exaggeration, a disproportion in detail that can, if skilfully executed, suggest both sympathy and mockery. The future of realism . . . may lie in the ease with which it can sustain the carefully timed commentary of humour.'[15]

This realism is not consistent throughout the whole work: it is there in the sexual episodes, at least by the criterion of obscenity, and in the *Cena*, but the exigencies of certain stock satiric themes (e.g. *captatio*, which even Horace did not try to make a realistic subject but introduced into a humorous dialogue between Ulysses and Teiresias) and Petronius' other literary aims such as parody and literary criticism militate against realism in the treatment of the legacy-hunters at Croton (124 *ad fin.* ff), in the episodes at sea (100 ff) or in 119 ff, where Eumolpus recites his unfinished *Carmen de Bello Civili* without any protest from Encolpius, who had earlier complained of his untimely poeticizing (90.3–4).

The realism, then, is prompted by, and so at the service and mercy of, two main factors. The first is the opportunistic choice of Menippean satire as a reaction against contemporary literary trends and a suitable vehicle for Petronius' literary interests; the second, which is not unconnected with the first, is the attraction this mode of writing had for someone of Petronius' psychological make-up and literary circumstances.

Where the satirist who uses realism, even in conjunction with other techniques, and the naturalistic novelists, whose realism is intended as a neutral reporting of life *as it really is*, seem to overlap is in their conception of realism. What unifies the realist tradition in any genre, and sets it off against the romantic, the heroic and the sentimental, is the belief that only the vulgar, the sordid and the sexual elements of life are truly real, that the rest is the humbug of the canting moralist. The feeling is well described by a modern writer, Mary McCarthy, as 'the denigration of the real' and is well illustrated in passage from one of her short stories:

He knew immediately that he was not meant to hear; these shrieks were being rung from a being against its will; yet in this fact, precisely, lay their power to electrify the attention. 'A dying woman screaming in the night,' the young man repeated musingly, as the cries stopped, at their very summit, as abruptly as they had started, leaving a pounding stillness, 'this is the actual; the actual in fact is *that which should not be witnessed.* The actual,' he defined, pronouncing the syllables slowly and distinctly in a pedagogical style, 'under which may be subsumed the street accident, the plane crash, the atrocity, is pornography.'[16]

Whatever the limiting judgements we may be forced to make on this heresy of the naïve realist, it seems clear that the elements of realism in Petronius conform to this conception of realism. *Nostalgie de la boue* would foster such an attitude and the psychosexual patterns we saw in the work would narrow still further the field of sexual 'realism' drawn upon. The literary defence in 132 is little more than a defence against the strictures of moralists and displays a very limited view of *quod facit populus*, even when we extend this to the vulgarity of Trimalchio's circle. Nor does the Epicurean defence of its moral rightness make any more acceptable the narrowness of the description of reality. Large parts of the *Satyricon* may therefore with good reason be described as a 'realistic' novel—with all this implies.

IV. *The* Satyricon *as Satire*

It may be argued that although this realism is a limitation in the novel which purports to represent the real world, yet for the satirist, whose object is to castigate and perhaps correct vice, folly or other aberration, it is an allowable and sometimes necessary way of writing, a way of writing which, in fact, may represent the satirist's vision of the world and may achieve the ostensible objects of satire. This, however, is no defence of Petronius, who is not a real satirist at all. His choice of form has been explained and although the themes such a choice entailed are used by him, they are not deployed as the true satirist deploys them. Petronius lacks the coherent moral standpoint from which satire ideally springs and the evidence for this is not far to seek.

To take some minor satirical themes first. The legacy-hunting episode is milked only for its humour, as far as we can judge, and for its adaptability to the picaresque adventures of Encolpius and his friends. The description of the business of Croton at 116 is purely conventional, and is seized upon by Eumolpus as the ideal opportunity to ensure them all an easy life. The satirical description of ladies who prefer slaves as lovers is given directly by Chrysis to the only repository of moral sentiment available in the *Satyricon*, but Encolpius nevertheless falls in love with Circe.

The episode which has the greatest claim to be truly satirical is the *Cena*; but certain points must be noted. First of all, the basic subject, Trimalchio, is so added to that the postulated satiric purpose recedes into the background and the section becomes an exuberant creation which exists in its own right, much as *The Pickwick Papers*, originally intended as a humorous text for Seymour's hunting sketches, took on the full-blown vitality of a self-subsistent work. As was mentioned above, this has even deceived scholars into postulating a fondness for Trimalchio or his real life original. What has happened, however, is that the satirical theme of the vulgarian's dinner party is now treated with a real novelist's verve, largely because the satirist's impulse is deficient in Petronius. There are further confirmations of this in the treatment of Trimalchio. To begin with, the whole standard evoked is that of taste. This can, of course, be a genuine satirical position, but Petronius undercuts its coherence by his depiction of Encolpius, who is deliberately and constantly revealed as an inadequate moral, or even aesthetic, commentator.

It is true that Trimalchio exemplifies fatuity and bad taste and that the lavish display of wealth without any aesthetic capacity for its proper use is both a natural target for an Arbiter of Elegance, and a traditional theme for satire. The hits are recorded by the repeated ironic stress on the words *lautitiae, elegantia* and their cognates (27.4, 31.8, 34.5, 34.8, etc.), but the record is also kept of Encolpius' own failings in this respect. Trimalchio's fatuity, part of which was shared by more august figures, is shown in his liking for charades, the rebus-game and such inferior entertainments as acrobats and horn-players and in his poor grasp of mythology and history.[17] But Encolpius' admiration of certain of Trimalchio's more novel vulgarities cancels his condemnation of the insipidities and his fear of being considered uncultured or not quite a gentleman cancels still more of his criticism.[18]

This ambivalence in Petronius' satire is symptomatic. It is as though he were struggling to be a novelist who depicts reality without moral comment (even though his decision as to what is *truly* real is itself a moral comment) rather than a satirist, whose whole object is castigation. But the force of literary tradition was too much for him and he was unable to free himself of the laws the satiric form imposed on him. This makes his satire half-hearted, his realism intermittent, and his attitude to his non-sexual themes ambivalent. This ambivalence seems so pervasive that even the use of disreputable characters for the introduction of literary and social criticism may be explained by it.

In sum, Petronius may be seen as a novelist *manqué*, a realistic novelist who had not freed himself from the necessities of his traditional form. Only in the *Cena* does he manage to transcend these limitations; elsewhere his literary opportunism has been responsible for the production of a *beau monstre* which belongs to no recognizable literary genre, except superficially. Apart from Trimalchio and his circle, even his characterization is at the mercy of his literary self-indulgence, and as a result the *Satyricon* for all its distinction of writing and originality of invention remains a work of art that lacks any real centre.

NOTES

The text quoted in this essay is that of Konrad Mueller (Basel, 1961). The numbers in brackets usually refer to chapters. I would like to acknowledge here the help I have derived from various discussions with J. G. Griffith, H. A. Mason, W. W. Robson, and K. F. C. Rose.

[1] The bibliography on this subject is enormous. Among more recent work, H. T. Rowell, 'The Gladiator Petraites and the Date of the *Satyricon*', *TAPA* 89 (1958), 14 ff, might be mentioned. H. C. Schnur has summarized the best of the economic arguments in 'The Economic Background of the *Satyricon*', *Latomus* 18 (1959), 790 ff. And the most recent and plausible of the attempts to date our portion of the work more closely is that of K. F. C. Rose, 'The Date of the *Satyricon*', *CQ* 12 (1962), 166 ff.

[2] Rose puts forward a good case for identifying this man with T. Petronius Niger and dating his consulship to A.D. 62.

[3] I might add here in view of certain recent attempts to overvalue him (cf. e.g. G. H. Gellie, 'A Comment on Petronius', *AUMLA* 10 (1959), 89 f), that I do not think he was a very good *poet*; although it must be granted that most of our examples of his verse are *vers d'occasion fictive*.

His verse, in fact, is what one would expect from rather reactionary poetic principles and one must be careful not to include in one's judgement some of the non-Petronian poems printed in many editions.

⁴ cf. Mario Praz, *The Romantic Agony* (1951), *passim*.

⁵ I accept the arguments of scholars such as Iannelli for Puteoli as the location of the *Cena*; the proximity of Petronius' villa at Cumae to the town allowed the satisfaction of a certain curiosity, which would be the ancient equivalent of our 'slumming'.

⁶ I have laid out in detail elsewhere the evidence for what follows ('The *Satiricon* of Petronius—Some Psycho-analytical Considerations', *American Imago* 18 (1961), 353–69); but as this journal is comparatively inaccessible, I have thought it advisable to summarize and add to some of the arguments and conclusions. I should like to add for those who may find such investigations distasteful the opening remarks of Freud to his study, *Leonardo da Vinci*:

'When psychoanalytic investigation, which usually contents itself with frail human material, approaches the great personages of humanity, it is not impelled to it by motives which are often imputed to it by laymen. It does not strive "to blacken the radiant and to drag the sublime into the mire"; it finds no satisfaction in diminishing the distance between the perfection of the great and the inadequacy of the ordinary objects. But it cannot help finding that everything is worthy of understanding that can be perceived through those prototypes, and it also believes that none is so big as to be ashamed of being subject to the laws which control the normal and morbid actions with the same strictness.'

(Authorized translation by A. A. Brill)

⁷ cf. the above article, p. 360, n. 6.

⁸ 'Instincts and their Vicissitudes' (1915), *Collected Papers*, Vol. IV (English Edition), p. 73.

⁹ O. Fenichel, *The Psychoanalytic Theory of Neurosis* (1945), p. 72. Note also Petronius' interest in Nero's private life (Tac. *Ann.* 16.18, quoted above).

¹⁰ 'Restriction and Transformations of Scopophilia in Psychoneurotics', *Selected Papers* (English Edition, 1949), p. 219.

¹¹ ibid., p. 186.

¹² See Fenichel, op. cit., p. 71.

Very often sadistic impulses are tied up with scopophilia: the individual wants to see something in order to destroy it (or to gain reassurance that the object is not yet destroyed). Often, looking itself is unconsciously thought of as a substitute for destroying ('I did not destroy it; I merely looked at it').

The significance for the passages cited needs no explanation.

It should be stressed that the psychoanalytical arguments here are not meant to prove that the author of *Satyricon* was a pathological case of either voyeurism or exhibitionism, or indeed that the *Satyricon* was some sort of catharsis for its author. All that is proved, I believe, granted our psychoanalytical premises, is the genuine autonomy of the author in chosing sexual material for his work, namely material which appealed to him and which was not forced upon him by social or literary considerations.

[13] Various lists of echoes and parallels may be found in G. Studer, *RhM* 2 (1843), 89–91; H. C. Schnur's dissertation, *The Age of Petronius Arbiter* (1957), pp. 123–34, and J. Gottschlich, *de parodiis Senecae apud Petronium* (1865)—cf., however, A. Collignon, *Etude sur Pétrone* (1892) 291–303.

[14] This realism has frequently been commented on. In fact, G. Bagnani has seen behind the creation of Trimalchio some living original, perhaps an ex-slave of Petronius' ('Trimalchio', *Phoenix* 8 (1954), 77), but, in fact, the less naturalistic elements used in the creation of Trimalchio tell against this, as well as qualifying our conception of Petronius as an ultra-modern realistic writer. For instance, topical references to Nero's court such as Otho's innovation, aped by Trimalchio, of anointing the guests' feet at dinner (70.8, cf. Pliny, *NH*, 13.22); the use of various traits belonging to contemporary or well-known figures to build up the bizarre central character: Claudius' famous *edictum de flatu* (Suet. *Claud.* 32.5) is mockingly paralleled at 47.4–6; Trimalchio has a mock funeral like Pacuvius (cf. Sen., *Ep.*, 12.8); his pretensions to learning resemble those of Calvisius Sabinus (cf. 48.4, 50.5 and Sen. Ep. 27.5), etc.

Much work has been devoted to the careful comparison of the dialects of the lower-class speakers with the Pompeian *graffiti* and to the investigation of their Greek elements. It is doubtful, however, whether Petronius would work with the scholarly care of a dialect cartographer. Something similar to Petronius' technique may be seen in D. H. Lawrence's *Lady Chatterley's Lover* (Penguin Books, 1960, pp. 104 ff), where Mrs. Bolton discusses the village with Clifford Chatterley. Compare with this, e.g. the conversation of Seleucus and Phileros (42, 43).

[15] Roger Shattuck, *The Banquet Years* (1961), p. 34.

[16] 'The Old Men' in *Cast a Cold Eye*, p. 147.

[17] cf. 41, 56, 53, 50, 52.

[18] cf. e.g. 41.

IS JUVENAL A CLASSIC?

An Introductory Essay

H. A. Mason

'EVERYTHING depends on the reality of a poet's classic character. If he is a dubious classic, let us sift him; if he is a false classic, let us explode him. But if he is a real classic, if his work belongs to the class of the very best (for this is the true and right meaning of the word *classic, classical*), then the great thing for us is to feel and enjoy his work as deeply as ever we can, and to appreciate the wide difference between it and all work which has not the same high character.'

After G. G. Ramsay had pronounced, in the introduction to the Loeb translation, that Juvenal is 'the greatest satirist, and one of the greatest moralists, of the world', it would seem an odd pretension for an amateur to suppose that any arguments he might put forward for contesting these two claims could serve to clarify serious thinking about Juvenal. At the same time, this remark of Ramsay's could not be made with any claim to critical authority by a mere specialist. For these assertions presuppose comparison of the Latin poet with all other moral satirists before Juvenal and after him down to the time of writing, and any such comparison could obviously not be made by a committee each member of which was a competent judge in only *one* of the relevant literatures. And if we inquire into the status of Juvenal as a *classic*, there is a further implication that, whoever proposes the sentence, the jury appealed to is the common sense of mankind.

It would nevertheless be an absurd pretension to put forward an account of Juvenal that contradicted the *consensus* of the scholars. After all, most of what occurs when an amateur reads a Latin author is the taking over of meanings established by learned commentators who have examined all the other contexts in which the author's words have come down to us. And even on matters of taste it seems reasonable to listen first to those who have made a special study of the author's manner and spirit. About Juvenal's merits, however, there is no scholarly *consensus*: the specialists do not speak with one voice. It would be easy to quote opinions from them showing that Juvenal's status as a classic is not securely established. Moreover, quite apart from the comparative merits of Juvenal among the world's moral satirists, there is no agreement about what might seem to be almost matters of *fact*: the qualities that mark Juvenal out as a poet distinct from other Latin poets.

The contention of this essay is that the characteristic qualities of Juvenal's art are such that he cannot be described as a classic of moral satire. To establish such a contention would clearly involve a vast European debate, which could not take place until common ground had been made to bring all the competent witnesses into effective opposition. In the present state of classical studies the prospect of setting up anything of this kind is remote. To judge by the standard works and recent essays on Juvenal written in the chief European languages, the learned authors all seem to exemplify the German phrase *aneinander vorbeireden*. While apparently addressing their colleagues across the national frontiers they have in fact no common set of critical presuppositions or standards.

If this is broadly true, it would not after all seem odd for the amateur to address some interrogatory remarks to the body of the learned. But he is in a very much happier position when he turns to those who may be styled in comparison with himself *beginners*. The principal object of this essay is to communicate delight, or to make faintly comprehensible what Dryden may have meant when he said of Juvenal, 'he gives me as much pleasure as I can bear'. It is because I think Ramsay's claim distracts attention from what is delightful in Juvenal that I have tried in my amateur way to demolish it. Moreover, delight breeds understanding: to relish Juvenal's real qualities is to gain in appreciation of an unfamiliar branch of satire, and when we see how it differs from the branch which the ordinary cultivated reader knows better, that of Boileau, Dryden, Pope and Johnson, we read these later authors with increased delight.

The only peculiarity I am conscious of displaying in this summary account of the pleasures obtainable from a reading of Juvenal is that while I have picked up innumerable hints from the scholars referred to above, my chief debts are to those modern satirists who enjoyed Juvenal but chose different paths. Nevertheless I would be prepared to claim that this special route is the most profitable one for developing the necessary *flair* to appreciate Juvenal's real qualities. I do not see how we can hope to become literary critics of any foreign poetry without first graduating as critics of the poetry that is nearest to us. The royal road to Juvenal is through profound enjoyment of the poetry of Eliot and Pound.

The amateur rightly diffident when addressing scholars may turn with equal happiness to his fellows and particularly to those who have made their own comparisons among the satirists of classical and modern times. Here I am conscious of parting company with those of my fellow-amateurs who see Juvenal as a neurotic sufferer from ill-treatment by Domitian; full of pent-up feelings all clamouring for simultaneous expression; with a prophet's diagnosis of the true ills of his times and a prophet's mission to set them right; deeply indignant, morally earnest, passionately sincere; simple-minded and literal on the whole; a man with something of a philosophy, though not a formal philosopher; and at the same time an admirable witness to what was really happening on the seamy side of Rome. To this false image, as it seems to me, I am not dogmatically but deliberately opposed. I shall, however, avoid the temptation to sharpen my opposition, since gentle persuasion is the only hopeful critical tool. It is a deplorable lapse in critical manners to attribute 'hostility' or 'prejudice', a mind closed to experience, to those who place the main accent in a different place than that which seems the only right place to ourselves. We should take a warning from recent differences of opinion about Milton. Here I assume that the debate is between amateurs in the sense of lovers, between those who say, 'I love my love with an A' and those who would substitute B or even Z.

There can be no debate, however, without common ground. To wean fellow-lovers of Juvenal from their cherished image, it will be necessary to go over the poems which seem most to favour this image. It is not part of my case that those with whom I disagree have overlooked the best poems of Juvenal. I am not proposing an alternative selection from the *œuvre*. But before engaging with the recognized masterpieces I should like to comment on one poem in which all the real qualities of Juvenal seem to me strikingly present, and so challenge those who believe in the 'false' image to a preliminary skirmish. It will be my contention that what holds good of the ninth satire is true of the third, the sixth and the tenth, the satires which seem to offer the best support for the account of Juvenal I shall attempt to discredit. I also think that this ninth satire is the best introduction for the unprejudiced beginner.

Here, however, I imagine the friendly expert remonstrating: 'Surely this is an odd way to introduce new readers to Juvenal? You have chosen a back entrance to the palace and one, too, you must confess, that leads through the offices, if not the very sewers and drains. It is not only for the sake of sixth-formers that there has never been a detailed commentary on it in English. You yourself would be unable to expound some parts of it in public.' The expert, however, would, I take it, concede that here we have Juvenal's art in the purest, most concentrated form. The particular advantage I wish to take by this beginning is to isolate these artistic qualities in a context which marks Juvenal off from any modern European writer.

My first contention is that Juvenal appears here without the faintest moral concern about the subject-matter he has chosen as the substratum of his poem. He never for one moment directs his attention to the verdict he would have to give on his hero if he had been an actual figure in Roman society. Juvenal's interest at no point overlaps with that of, say, Marcel Proust dealing with the sexual monsters of his day. Nor, on the other hand, can we conclude from this poem that Juvenal in private life would have been either fascinated with or cynical about such abominable behaviour. The effect of the poem is to direct our attention into a region remote from that of the social commentator.

Why then, the rejoinder might come, does Juvenal abound and even seem to delight in the abundance of pointed obscenities? My second contention is that the key to Juvenal's art lies in the study of Martial. The two poets appeal to the same taste and presuppose the same habits in their listening and reading public. Since our taste and habits are quite different from theirs, it will be necessary to define some of the respects in which their world is separated by a gulf from ours.

We should not, however, suppose, when we find Martial and Juvenal making poems out of matters of obscenity, that their audience consisted of dissolute rakes or perverts without moral sense or taste. The gulf between them and us lies in their attitude towards such poems. That the pervert offended against a clearly held social and moral standard can be seen from a short epigram of Martial's (9.63) which depends on the two meanings of *purus* ('bright' and 'pure') and the name, Phoebus, the bright, of the victim:

> ad cenam inuitant omnes te, Phoebe, cinaedi.
> mentula quem pascit, non, puto, purus homo est.

Purebright, you are a welcome guest at the tables of all the pathics in town: a man who pays for his dinner by satisfying *them* may be bright but he cannot, I think, be called pure.

Yet what is puzzling is that Martial supposed his poems would be acceptable to men of strict life while producing upon them the extreme effects of pornography:

> o quotiens rigida pulsabis pallia uena
> sis grauior Curio Fabricioque licet! (11.16)

That Martial was correct in his supposition is shown by two letters (4.14 and 5.3) of Pliny the Younger, the soul of Roman gentility. In both letters his defence of obscenity in his poems is the same: 'If you find any of them rather too *risqué*, I must ask you to recall from your wide reading the names of those famous men of a pronounced serious cast of mind who wrote little poems of this kind in which they not only dared to treat scabrous themes but were not afraid to use the naked language of obscenity.' 'Nor do I mind shocking people who think it odd that a man of my character, as they say, should compose indecent poems, since they presumably do not know that men of great learning, men of the most serious cast of mind, men of holy life even, have been in the habit of writing verse of this kind.'

For such a claim to be possible, this resort to verse on obscene matters must have contained an element of play and an element of convention. When we read a few of the obscene epigrams we can imagine something analogous in our conditions. But how are we to account for the Romans' apparent relish of the abominable? In this perplexity we may as well turn to the explanation given by

Martial himself, that the indulgence claimed for his topics was that licensed by the Saturnalia:

> uersus hos tamen esse tu memento
> Saturnalicios, Apollinaris:
> mores non habet hic meos libellus. (11.15)

These poems are meant to be read in the spirit of the Saturnalia. Do not conclude that I am licentious because my verses are.

More apposite for us when reading Juvenal is Martial's assertion in the introduction to the eighth book of his epigrams that 'men of the highest position and the strictest morals have written epigrams in language aiming at the freedom of the mime', and the amusing point in 3.86:

> ne legeres partem lasciui, casta, libelli,
>   praedixi et monui: tu tamen, ecce, legis.
> sed si Panniculum spectas et, casta, Latinum,
>   (non sunt haec mimis inprobiora) lege.

I warned you that the epigrams in this book after No. 67 were not fit for respectable married women, and now I catch you reading as far as here. Still, if you, a respectable married woman, go to the mime to see Panniculus and Latinus—since my poems are not more indecent than mimes—you may . . . read on.

Although we should never take Juvenal literally, we may gather from a passage in the sixth satire how great a licence Martial was claiming for himself in asking Caesar (1.4) to read his poems in the same frame of mind as that in which he went to see the actor Latinus playing opposite Thymele, for there, Juvenal asserts, Thymele, the professional actress, used to miming to the life the part of Leda receiving the swan, learns new refinements for her act when she watches one female spectator of the supple Bathyllus losing control of herself and hears another moaning with desire as if the whole mime were going on in real life.

That the Romans could tolerate the mime is not so astonishing as the claim that poems dealing in the stock situations of the mime could be ranked among the imperishable monuments of art. Martial clearly thought his epigrams a more serious form of art than what currently passed for literature. Since I think Juvenal felt the same hostility to the current literary fashions and shared

Martial's view of what constituted serious art, it is worth quoting
a specimen of Martial's artistic manifesto:

> nescit, crede mihi, quid sint epigrammata, Flacce,
>   qui tantum lusus ista iocosque uocat.
> ille magis ludit qui scribit prandia saeui
>   Tereos aut cenam, crude Thyesta, tuam,
> aut puero liquidas aptantem Daedalon alas,
>   pascentem Siculas aut Polyphemon ouis.
> a nostris procul est omnis uesica libellis,
>   Musa nec insano syrmate nostra tumet.
> . . . 'illa tamen laudant omnes, mirantur, adorant.'
> confiteor: laudant illa sed ista legunt. (4.49)

If Statius or anybody else has been telling you, Flaccus, that my
epigrams are nothing but light verse, he doesn't know what he is
talking about. Let *me* tell you that *he* is far less serious than I am when
he composes wordy poems about the dinner served up to that inhuman
monster, Tereus, or the meal Thyestes found so indigestible, or of
Daedalus fitting out his son with wings that would not stand the
critical temperature, or of Polyphemus behaving like a Sicilian shepherd. *My* poems are quite free from surplusage and my style from the
swelling bombast of our modern tragedians. 'Yes, but his epics and
tragedies get praise, universal admiration, religious respect.' They may
get praise, but they don't get read.

In an effort to grasp in a summary way the positive and negative claims Martial and Juvenal were making for their art we
might turn to the analogy of Donne and Jonson. There are more
than verbal similarities in the epitaph Carew wrote on Donne:
this, for instance, will give us something of the spirit:

> But thou art gone, and thy strict lawes will be
> Too hard for Libertines in Poetrie.
> They will repeale the goodly exil'd traine
> Of gods and goddesses, which in thy just raigne
> Were banish'd nobler Poems, now, with these
> The silenc'd tales o'th'Metamorphoses
> Shall stuffe their lines, and swell the windy Page . . .

And if we turn to another epigram (10.4), where Martial returns
to the attack on the contemporary vogue of mythological subjects,
and stress this line:

> quid te uana iuuant miserae ludibria chartae?

What pleasure or profit can you derive from poetry more worthless
than the waste paper it is written on?

it is fair to gloss it with D. H. Lawrence's remark: 'But if you believe me, that *Golden Journey to Samarcand* only took place on
paper—no matter who went to Asia Minor.'

In this epigram and in 8.3 Martial sets out the claim that I
would also make for Juvenal that by his wit he was bringing poetry closer to reality:

> hoc lege, quod possit dicere uita 'meum est'.
> non hic Centauros, non Gorgonas Harpyiasque
> inuenies: hominem pagina nostra sapit.

Why do you refuse to touch my epigrams that have real life written all
over them? You can search my book from cover to cover and you
won't find a single Centaur, Gorgon or Harpy. What you *will* find
there is the authentic taste and smell of Man.

With this we may compare the following from 8.3:

> at tu Romano lepidos sale tinge libellos:
> adgnoscat mores uita legatque suos.

which, with an eye on the context, we may take in the spirit of the
following: 'Leave high-flown themes to pedantic moralists and
salt your epigrams with urban wit, so that life may see herself in
them and know her habits for what they are.'

These remarks thrown out in advance of any proof may at least
serve to guide our attention in the direction Juvenal is inviting us
to take. Juvenal, that is to say, is far less interested in presenting
a social reality than in extracting opportunities for witty excur-
sions. Naevolus is a stock figure and is allowed a minimal farcical
existence as a sexual maid-of-all-work in the house of a married
passive homosexual. But the life of the poem is in the bizarre effect of putting into his mouth remarks quite out of keeping with
his overt activity. The joke requires this minimum presence of
sexual monstrosity (or abnormal dexterity) but the strokes of wit
come when Naevolus speaks as if he were Martial or Juvenal himself. No attempt at drama is offered. The dialogue merely gives
an occasion for *declamation* on a number of loosely-related topics.
There is a light connecting thread in that this satire parodies one

of Juvenal's favourite forms for satire, the exposition of a *propositum uitae*. But nobody could seriously put Naevolus on a par with the Umbricius of the third satire. The only serious part of the *propositum* is that which refers to Juvenal's and Martial's perennial personal predicament, the state of *paupertas* or genteel poverty. Naevolus is something like a music-hall comic whose 'character' is flexible enough to act as a support for a repertoire of unconnected jokes and disparate social reflections.

It would help the reader to grasp the nature of Juvenal's art if his poems were printed in sections with gaps to mark the close of one section and the beginning of the next. The tone of the first section, in which Juvenal addresses Naevolus, I can only describe by resorting to French—it is *gouailleur*: at least it seems to me to be nearer amused banter than anything else. It is not easy to be sure of the tone since this section is a highly-worked-up declamation. By this I mean that, though formally addressed to Naevolus, it is declaimed at an invisible audience of bystanders, to whom Naevolus is invisible and needs describing. Juvenal gives us three images to lead up to the question: 'why all these wrinkles on your forehead, Naevolus?' They are, characteristically, as I hope to show later, visual images. The first comes from the world of art: a popular study of pain in Greco-Roman sculpture was the fate of Marsyas, who had in legend been punished for trying to rival Apollo as a musician. The third may come from real life: the dejection and exasperation of a man offering easy money loans but unable to find takers. In between Juvenal places an image from Martial: the look of surprise and shame when a man is caught performing a specified indecent act with a whore. This image appears to come from stock, perhaps from a farce. Do these three images make a composite portrait? I don't think so, or even that they were meant to. They strike me as three separate ways of fixing Naevolus in our minds as a stock buffoon. Yet immediately after this, Naevolus is described as a Martial, a wit and a Roman wit. Then we are switched back to the outer man, to the loss of his former sleekness and the exaggerated seediness of his present exterior. After that come two lines of pure Juvenal, which read as if he had completely forgotten where he was: they might be a fragment from the passage on old age in the tenth poem. They give us the chief ingredient in Juvenal's wit, *the belittling remark in the style of epic grandeur*. This is what is so hard to catch in translation, and so hard to describe, for the effect is unlike the corresponding use of epic by Boileau, Dryden or Pope. This is the principal innovation of Juvenal on Martial's art. Martial, too, often gets analogous effects by weaving coarse matter on a delicate elegiac warp. Juvenal seems to have found the epic style more congenial. It is a complex effect, for it both mocks and belittles the epic style and raises the trivial or sordid subject only to let it fall lower than ever. As I hope to discuss this aspect of Juvenal's wit later on, I will here merely quote the lines:

> quid macies aegri ueteris, quem tempore longo
> torret quarta dies olimque domestica febris?

Juvenal continues to address Naevolus as a figure from Martial, a combination, as it were, of Don Juan for the ladies and equally enterprising with their husbands. Naevolus takes this last fling, which crowns the speech, neither as an insult nor a compliment. He replies in his puppet rôle of the utterly professional prostitute: 'Yes, that's me, and think of the money you earn!' Or, 'It's a good way of life for a man on the make, but I am unlucky in it.' Then he suddenly changes into the man of taste. The wages of sin are apparently the same as the wages of Martial's literary labours: a Gallic cloak, for instance. That this stood for the typical perquisite of a 'client' we may see from Persius (1.54):

> scis comitem horridulum trita donare lacerna

and Horace (*Ep.* 1.19.38):

> tritae munere uestis

and Martial himself, as in 12.72.4:

> paruaque sed tritae praemia certa togae.

The similarity between Martial and Naevolus is even closer if we take the former's deprecating reference to a garment in 4.19: 'This shaggy nursling of a weaver on the Seine . . . far from elegant, but useful in December, we send you . . .', and compare it with Naevolus: 'Every now and then you get a shaggy cloak, coarse in texture, tastelessly dyed, and crudely woven on a French weaver's loom, but it serves as a winter overcoat . . .'. It is characteristic of Juvenal when he is borrowing from Martial—even, it must be admitted, when borrowing obscenity—to carry the point a little further or to give the joke an extra twist. Naevolus also resembles Martial when he speaks of the second item in his wages, silverware. In fact both these articles were cadged for by Martial in a single epigram (10.14): 'When winter came, did you send me a cloak? When did I get from you half a pound's weight of silver ware?'

Then come four lines, again of the purest Juvenal. Naevolus reveals his philosophical side and blames fate for his ill luck, for fate alone, he feels, is a powerful enough agency to account for the failure of his incomparable equipment, personal advantages which bring the saliva to the lips of the susceptible beholder—and here again Juvenal outdoes Martial in the particularity with which he stamps the phrase—charms which cause the pathic to besiege Naevolus with love letters:

> blandae adsidue densaeque tabellae
> sollicitent

—the verse enacts the meaning. And Juvenal crowns this passage with one of his wittiest classical parodies. Naevolus quotes a line in Greek from the *Odyssey*: 'It is dangerous to leave naked weapons lying about, they have magnetic power to allure men to use them.' But Naevolus substitutes for the *naked weapons* at the end of the line the surprise-word *pathics*.

Naevolus in turn delivers a speech on the theme of the monstrosity of avarice in his perverted patron. He speaks as if his own relation to the patron were purely mercenary, and mechanical rather than physical. The speech turning on material rewards glides into a piece of literary nature description. I call it literary for two reasons: the matter is borrowed from Martial and Persius and the composition seems to have been inspired as much if not more by the pleasure of placing and caressing the proper names than by the desire to evoke the country where the names were found. The contrivance of such delicate oases—quite out of character—is certainly piquant, but surely their contrivance should put us on our guard against attributing simple-mindedness to Martial and Juvenal? Their very success makes translation impossible, but a 'crib' will serve to point the parallel between Martial and Naevolus: here first is Martial (10.74):

> non . . . Apulos uelim campos;
> non Hybla, non me spicifer capit Nilus,
> nec quae paludes delicata Pomptinas
> ex arce cliui spectat uua Setini.

As a reward for my doubtless trumpery poems, I do not ask for the plains of Apulia, nor am I taken with the thought of Hybla, nor all the corn in the Nile region, nor the delicate grapes of Setinum, which from the crest of the hill look down on the Pomptine marshes.

and here is Naevolus:

Speak up, you never-satisfied lecher, to whom are you going to make a present of all those mountains, all those estates in Apulia, so wide an area of pasture that the kite grows weary in flying over it? The soil of Trifolium enriches you with its fertile vines and the crest of the hill that looks down on Cumae and the unpeopled slopes of Gaurus.

> te Trifolinus ager fecundis uitibus implet
> suspectumque iugum Cumis et Gaurus inanis . . .

The reader who persists in finding a feeling for nature here might test whether he is not guilty of anachronism by comparing this with the poet Gray's fragment beginning

> Nec procul infelix se tollit in aethera Gaurus . . .

We now come upon another side of Juvenal's wit. So far Naevolus has been speaking as if before a judge in a divorce court and as if confronting his fraudulent ex-partner. This manner of speaking, to reach its height, requires a further element, the extreme situation. *Juvenal never triumphs without hyperbole*, as Boileau noted:

> Juvenal élevé dans les cris de l'Ecole
> Poussa jusqu'à l'excez sa mordante hyperbole.

To crown the speech, Naevolus reveals that—such is the love he bears him—he had also consented to father children on his patron's wife. There being no possibility of capping this, Juvenal changes the subject to the danger of gossiping about the misdoings of the rich. I cannot help suspecting that this transition was written to lead up to a wonderful piece of hyperbole on the theme: the rich can have no secrets. But before this bravura piece Juvenal inserts a touch of his finest wit. 'Ah, Corydon, Corydon', he says to Naevolus, recalling Virgil's second eclogue, where the youthful shepherd longs for his Alexis. This is more than a mere literary allusion. It is more, too, than the simple contrast between the sordid 'reality' of Naevolus' charms and the ideal beauty of Corydon, the sort of contrast exploited by Eliot in *The Waste Land*. A hint of the complexity may be obtained by looking at

Marvell, who went for his own purposes to this pastoral poem and made of it something that both criticizes the artificiality of the pastoral mode and benefits by being incidentally parasitic on it. Marvell's witty effect is obtained by forcing our minds to play between art and life, between, for instance, the literary pathos and

> Thestylis et rapido fessis messoribus aestu
> alia serpyllumque herbas contundit olentis,

the lively reality of the villagers out mowing:

> With whistling Sithe, and Elbow strong,
> These Massacre the Grass along:
> While one, unknowing, carves the *Rail*,
> Whose yet unfeather'd Quils her fail.
> The Edge all bloody from its Breast
> He draws, and does his stroke detest;
> Fearing the Flesh untimely mow'd
> To him a Fate as black forbode.
>
> But bloody *Thestylis*, that waites
> To bring the mowing Camp their Cates,
> Greedy as Kites has trust it up,
> And forthwith means on it to sup . . .

The reflections that arise when we allow the two situations of Naevolus and Corydon to develop side by side may not be the same for every mind. Taken with the other jibes at Virgil's eclogues in Juvenal, we may be inclined to see in this allusion a further criticism of the homosexual love among literary shepherds and a Johnsonian distaste for the mode. But even so, Juvenal was clearly fascinated by the beauty of the closing passage of the eclogue and the sharp contrast as well as the similarity in the *mores* of the eclogue and his own chosen mime. He wanted his readers to remember when he tells Naevolus that he will easily find another patron that Virgil had so consoled Corydon: 'The tawny lioness pursues the wolf, the wolf the goat, the wanton goat chases the flowering lucerne, Corydon chases you, Alexis. Each is drawn along by his peculiar pleasure. . . . Love consumes me with fire, for who can put a stop to love?—Ah, Corydon, Corydon, what madness has got hold of you? . . . you will find another Alexis if this one scorns you.' Another characteristic stroke comes after what I have called the bravura piece: 'There are several

reasons for leading a decent life: the best is that you then don't
have to bother what the servants say.' What is characteristic is the
deflating context given to the moral statement. We shall be meeting
with many instances in the further exploration of Juvenal's poems.
The best known is: 'The greatest reverence is owed to youth—if
you are getting ready to do something foul'. This type of wit is
dramatized by putting into the mouth of the abominable Naevolus
the kind of moral reflection people like to write in albums or on
sundials: 'Give me some advice: tell me what to do now I have
come to grief and wasted my time. For the flower of youth hastes
fast away and the little remainder of my miserable life will soon be
over. While we drink and call for garlands, perfumes, girls, old
age creeps on us unawares. 'There's no need to worry,' Juvenal
replies. 'As long as Rome stands on these seven hills, there will be
no lack of clientele. Maintain your diet of aphrodisiacs and every
ship, every cart will bring to the metropolis from all the corners of
the world its load of those who make the international sign of their
fellowship:

> qui digito scalpunt uno caput.'

The point of this vivid periphrasis is brought out by Augusto
Serafini, who in his study of Juvenal's satire refers us to an allusion to Pompey by Licinius Calvus:

> Magnus, quem metuunt omnes, digito caput uno
> scalpit: quid credas hunc sibi uelle? uirum.

Juvenal gives Naevolus the last word and once again makes him
behave in a way appropriate to Martial or Juvenal himself. For
he pays religious respect to his Lares and prays to be saved from
starvation. But as his prayer develops it becomes increasingly
ambitious. First he asks for the sort of establishment Juvenal and
Martial were angling for, then he adds craftsmen to paint and
sculpt and make *objets d'art* for him. The penultimate point of
the poem is again from Martial, who had written: 'You can't call
a man *pauper* who has nothing at all'. Naevolus says: 'When shall
I be rich enough to call myself respectably poor? Never, I fear.'
The poem ends with a lovely touch from the *Odyssey*: 'When I pray
to the Goddess Fortune, she fills her ears with wax from the ship
that survived the sirens' song only by making the rowers deaf.'

The last line of the poem, no doubt adapted from Propertius 3.12.34:

> Sirenum surdo remige adisse lacus

might have come from a serious work:

> quae Siculos cantus ecfugit remige surdo.

In thus lightly touching on what would strike any reader who consented to start on a study of Juvenal by reading the ninth poem, I hope to have provided the ideal introduction to what many have thought his finest poem, the sixth. At the same time I have indicated the topics I propose to discuss and which will give shape to this essay. First I hope to have listed the qualities that distinguish Juvenal as a poet and to have hinted at the peculiarities of Juvenal as a satirist. In what follows I shall try to substantiate the claim that if Juvenal is a classic he is a classic of wit; that this wit is obtained both by detachment from 'reality' and complicity in the 'unreal' substratum of obscene or scandalous subject-matter. In particular I hope to show that he was more interested in literature than social conditions and that he lacks any consistent standpoint or moral coherence. Indeed his whole art consists in opportunism and the surprise effects obtainable from deliberate inconsistency. To make this account plausible I have as far as possible allowed the poems to make their impact first as wholes. Although on re-reading I believe that what I claim to be characteristic of Juvenal would be found in every part, in the hope of carrying the beginner with me I shall discuss only what emerges from each poem as its main point.

Even if it be granted that the ninth poem could not have been written if Juvenal had been preoccupied with any of the moral issues which would have arisen had he been interested in the human situation of the poem, it still remains true that in other poems apparent evidence of moral interest is to be found. Some account must therefore be given of this evidence before the description of the ninth poem can be taken as typical or representative. It will be agreed, I think, that Juvenal's tenth is among those that have been thought to contain evidence of moral insight and moral interest. Dryden reports that this poem was recommended by a bishop to his clergy for use in sermons. In choosing this from among the 'moral' poems I have been guided by further interests. For Samuel Johnson based his great poem on this work and Johnson's poem is clearly one of the kind we want to bring Juvenal to a decisive test. For it will guide us in judging Juvenal to have a poem which takes up the same topics and is undoubtedly the work of a serious moralist. A further reason for taking *The Vanity of Human Wishes* is that it illustrates Johnson's sense of the essential features of Juvenal's style as they are given in his remarks on Dryden's translation of Juvenal. There Johnson spoke of the *dignity* of the original and defined the peculiarity of Juvenal as 'a mixture of gaiety and *stateliness*, of pointed sentences and declamatory *grandeur*'. I have put into italics the epithets that seem to me questionable.

But first as to the moral interest. Byron's remark, 'How true!' which he applied to both poems, in my opinion applies only to Johnson's. And the impression of truth I get from Johnson's poem comes from the feeling that I am there in the presence of an incomparably finer moral interest, which reveals itself to me locally as a much greater intellectual grasp: Johnson's mind is really gripping the theme and forcing it home. Juvenal does not exhibit this, the most precious form of intelligence, at all. Compare, for instance, from the opening, Juvenal's cliché *erroris nebula* and the empty antithesis *toga . . . militia* with the powerful treatment in Johnson. The beginner may prefer to compare Dryden with Johnson, but Dryden has ignored 'the mist of error':

> Look round the Habitable World, how few
> Know their own Good, or knowing it, pursue.
> How void of Reason are our Hopes and Fears!
> What in the Conduct of our Life appears
> So well design'd, so luckily begun,
> But, when we have our wish, we wish undone?
> Whole Houses, of their whole Desires possest,
> Are often Ruin'd, at their own Request.
> In Wars, and Peace, things hurtful we require,
> When made Obnoxious to our own Desire.
> With Laurels some have fatally been Crown'd; ⎱
> Some who the depths of Eloquence have found, ⎰
> In that unnavigable Stream were Drown'd.
> The Brawny Fool, who did his Vigour boast,
> In that Presumeing Confidence was lost:

The brawny fool is the legendary strong man of antiquity, Milo, who, as Roscommon put it,

> met his end
> Wedg'd in the Timber which he strove to rend

—a reference omitted by Johnson, who wrote:

> Let observation with extensive view,
> Survey mankind, from China to Peru;
> Remark each anxious toil, each eager strife,
> And watch the busy scenes of crouded life;
> Then say how hope and fear, desire and hate,
> O'erspread with snares the clouded maze of fate,
> Where wav'ring man, betray'd by vent'rous pride,
> To tread the dreary paths without a guide,
> As treach'rous phantoms in the mist delude,
> Shuns fancied ills, or chases airy good;
> How rarely reason guides the stubborn choice,
> Rules the bold hand, or prompts the suppliant voice;
> How nations sink, by darling schemes oppress'd,
> When vengeance listens to the fool's request.
> Fate wings with ev'ry wish th'afflictive dart,
> Each gift of nature, and each grace of art,
> With fatal heat impetuous courage glows,
> With fatal sweetness elocution flows,
> Impeachment stops the speaker's pow'rful breath,
> And restless fire precipitates on death.

There is a similar effort to clothe the merely verbal antithesis with meaning in the passage corresponding to Juvenal's single line: 'Democritus used to laugh at the worries, joys and tears of the mob', which gave Johnson an opportunity for:

> Attentive truth and nature to descry,
> And pierce each scene with philosophic eye.
> To thee were solemn toys or empty shew,
> The robes of pleasure and the veils of woe:
> All aid the farce, and all thy mirth maintain,
> Whose joys are causeless, or whose griefs are vain.

Although these are minor instances, they show that Johnson had abundance of matter close at hand. But, of course, the supreme examples of intellectual grasp are seen in the construction of the

famous portraits of Wolsey, Charles and the general characters
not attached to a name.

> In full-blown dignity, see Wolsey stand,
> Law in his voice, and fortune in his hand:
> To him the church, the realm, their pow'rs consign,
> Thro' him the rays of regal bounty shine,
> Turn'd by his nod the stream of honour flows,
> His smile alone security bestows:
> Still to new heights his restless wishes tow'r,
> Claim leads to claim, and pow'r advances pow'r;
> Till conquest unresisted ceas'd to please,
> And rights submitted, left him none to seize.
> At length his sov'reign frowns—the train of state
> Mark the keen glance, and watch the sign to hate.
> Where-e'er he turns he meets a stranger's eye,
> His suppliants scorn him, and his followers fly;
> At once is lost the pride of aweful state,
> The golden canopy, the glitt'ring plate,
> The regal palace, the luxurious board,
> The liv'ried army, and the menial lord.
> With age, with cares, with maladies oppress'd,
> He seeks the refuge of monastic rest.
> Grief aids disease, remember'd folly stings,
> And his last sighs reproach the faith of kings.

In considering Wolsey, it is hard to separate the two aspects of
Johnson's art, the intelligent ordonnance and the stately tone. We
can say that one aspect makes us see the portrait as a masterly
summary of history or of drama with all the organs preserved; the
five acts of the tragedy, as it were, are all present and the connection between them clear down to the last act, where

> Grief aids disease, remember'd folly stings,
> And his last sighs reproach the faith of kings.

This, however, is the lesser of the aspects. Johnson was not content to give us merely the Wolsey of history or of Shakespeare's
play. He has created a *poetic colossus*, as we become aware when
we feel how felicitous was the change to 'near the steeps of fate'
from 'by the Steps of fate':

> For why did Wolsey near the steeps of fate,
> On weak foundations raise th' enormous weight?

> Why but to sink beneath misfortune's blow,
> With louder ruin to the gulphs below?

If we look back to discover how Johnson has managed to create this effect of a colossus, we find it diffused over the whole passage, but there is one line in which the suggestion is peculiarly vivid:

> Turn'd by his nod the stream of honour flows . . .

When we recall the phrase 'the king is the fountain of honour' it is hard not to see Wolsey as an enormous edifice spouting water now in this direction now in that. This tendency, however, is checked and diverted inwards, for Johnson is inviting us to look rather on the exercise and display of moral qualities, and it is only when Wolsey is fallen that the material accoutrements are brought in:

> At once is lost the pride of aweful state,
> The golden canopy, the glitt'ring plate,
> The regal palace, the luxurious board,
> The liv'ried army, and the menial lord.

and here the adjectives are pointing the moral of the scene. The direction of our interest is inward to the activity on the stage of our own minds.

Here we have the essential contrast between Johnson and Juvenal, for Juvenal gives us in his Sejanus a *literal* colossus and his effects are mainly for the outer eye. Macaulay for this reason preferred Juvenal. 'The couplets in which the fall of Wolsey is described, though lofty and sonorous, are feeble when compared with the wonderful lines which bring before us all Rome in tumult on the day of the fall of Sejanus, the laurels on the doorposts, the white bull stalking towards the Capitol, the statues rolling down from their pedestals, the flatterers of the disgraced minister running to see him dragged with a hook through the streets, and to have a kick at his carcase before it is hurled into the Tiber.'

That this is an over-simplified and over-dramatic account of the passage I shall try to show by contrasting Ben Jonson's translations in *Sejanus*—which correspond with Macaulay—and Dryden's version, which, though faulty, is in my view more faithful to Juvenal's *tone*. Jonson gives us his first translation in rather literal English:

And now, the second face of the whole world,
The partner of the empire, hath his image
Rear'd equall with Tiberius.

This is from the first scene. The bulk of the Juvenal passage is, of course, reserved for the climax, the fall of Sejanus in Act V. Since Jonson's distribution of the text among the speakers is perfunctory, it will be doing no violence to ignore the dramatic form and present the passage as a narration by a single voice.

Crowne all our doores with bayes, and let an oxe
With gilded hornes, and garlands, straight be led
Vnto the capitoll, and sacrific'd
To Ioue, for Caesars safety.
Let all the traytors titles be defac'd,
His images, and statues be pull'd downe,
His chariot-wheeles be broken, and the legs
Of the poore horses, that deserued naught,
Let them be broken too.

Jonson then moralizes on Fortune's wheel, and borrows another piece of Juvenal, again without digesting it into English:

Fortune, thou hadst no deitie, if men
Had wisedome: we haue placed thee so high,
By fond beliefe in thy felicitie.

Then follows another bit of translation:

Now great Seianus, you that aw'd the state,
And sought to bring the nobles to your whip,
That would be Caesars tutor, and dispose
Of dignities and offices! . . .
                          now, you lie as flat,
As was your pride aduanc'd.

The actual scene of Juvenal's poem is given by Jonson without pretence of drama, as a narration. Terentius enters and describes how the people turned against Sejanus:

. . . like so many mastiues, biting stones,
As if his statues now were sensiue growne
Of their wild furie, first, they teare them downe:
Then fastning ropes, drag them along the streets,
Crying in scorne, this, this was that rich head
Was crown'd with gyrlands, and with odours, this

That was in Rome so reuerenced! Now
The fornace, and the bellowes shall to worke,
The great Seianus crack, and piece, by piece,
Drop i' the founders pit . . .
The whilst, the Senate, at the temple of Concord,
Make haste to meet againe, and thronging cry,
Let vs condemne him, tread him downe in water,
While he doth lie vpon the banke; away:
Where some, more tardie, cry vnto their bearers,
He will be censur'd ere we come, runne knaues;
And vse that furious diligence, for feare
Their bond-men should informe against their slacknesse,
And bring their quaking flesh vnto the hooke:
The rout, they follow with confused voyce,
Crying, they'are glad, say they could ne're abide him;
Enquire, what man he was? what kind of face?
What beard he had? what nose? what lips? protest,
They euer did presage h'would come to this:
They neuer thought him wise, nor valiant: aske
After his garments, when he dies? what death?
And not a beast of all the herd demands,
What was his crime? or, who were his accusers?
Vnder what proofe, or testimonie, he fell?
There came (sayes one) a huge, long, worded letter
From Capreae against him. Did there so?
O, they are satisfied, no more. Alas!
They follow fortune, and hate men condemn'd,
Guiltie, or not. But, had Seianus thriu'd
In his designe, and prosperously opprest
The old Tiberius, then, in that same minute,
These very raskals, that now rage like furies,
Would haue proclaim'd Seianus emperour.

There is an attractive freshness about this that makes it in-
finitely preferable to the stale language of Gifford. But it represents only the *surface* of Juvenal. It is an abstraction from the
text. What is absent from Jonson is Juvenal's *wit*. My contention
is that the wit is of the essence, not something tacked on, but
something that determines how we are to take everything else.
Dryden, I think, felt this, and supplied the deficiency in his own
way. But Juvenal's wit is not Dryden's: there is something very
much of the Restoration, as he himself admits, in Dryden's translation. Dryden's peculiar flavour is playful flippancy: it crops up

frequently enough to give its tone to the whole. For instance, an element in the Sejanus scene omitted by Jonson is the effect of the fall on one of his supporters:

> I met *Brutidius* in a Mortal fright;
> He's dipt for certain, and plays least in sight.

Samuel Johnson was right to complain of a want of dignity here. Occasionally Dryden makes Juvenal sound trivial:

> For Fame he pray'd, but let th' Event declare
> He had no mighty penn'worth of his Pray'r.

or, if not trivial, merely fooling. Take this, of Priam's death:

> His last Effort before *Jove's* Altar tries,
> A Souldier half, and half a Sacrifice.

What I think the reader would agree to call the Restoration note comes out well in the following passage:

> But your *Endymion*, your smooth, Smock-fac'd boy,
> Unrivall'd, shall a Beauteous Dame enjoy:
> Not so: One more Salacious, Rich, and Old,
> Out-bids, and buys her Pleasure for her Gold:
> Now he must Moil, and Drudge, for one he loaths,
> She keeps him High, in Equipage, and Cloaths:
> She Pawns her Jewels, and her Rich Attire,
> And thinks the Workman worthy of his Hire.

This is genuine creation: Juvenal has been transported to London, but he has suffered in the carriage. This comes out even more plainly in the passage where Silanus is forced into a mock marriage with Messalina and is ruined whether he consents or refuses:

> In this moot case, your Judgment: To refuse
> Is present Death, besides the Night you lose.
> If you consent, 'tis hardly worth your pain;
> A day or two of Anxious Life you gain:
> Till lowd Reports through all the Town have past,
> And reach the Prince: For Cuckolds hear the last.
> Indulge thy Pleasure, Youth, and take thy swing;
> For not to take, is but the self same thing;
> Inevitable Death before thee lies;
> But looks more kindly through a Ladies Eyes.

What we want, then, to characterize Juvenal's art aright, is neither the weighty point of Samuel Johnson, nor the simple directness of Ben Jonson, nor the affable irreverence of Dryden. Yet of the three Dryden seems to me to bring out best the keynote of Juvenal's poem. Juvenal's attitude towards his theme is complex, and I shall be doing injustice to it in splitting it up into discussible aspects. Yet this is merely a temporary device of criticism, for after attending to the elements in separation, we return to the poem and the act of re-reading restores the original complexity with (I hope) increased consciousness and hence enhanced appreciation of the complexity.

What none of the English versions supplies is the harsh belittling sarcasm or contemptuous animus which Juvenal directs against his figures. Here, from abundant examples, I select a few. Ben Jonson left out Juvenal's characteristic deflation after the huge 'build-up' of Sejanus. In the Latin every single word is working:

> iam strident ignes, iam follibus atque caminis
> ardet adoratum populo caput et crepat ingens
> Seianus: deinde ex facie toto orbe secunda . . .

Now the flames hiss as the heat is intensified by bellows: the furnace is stoked until the people's godhead glows red-hot and the huge colossus cracks, Sejanus, I mean! And now the second most important personage in the Roman Empire . . .

(what can come now? what greater climax has the poet in store?)

is turned into little brass jars, frying pans, foot pans, piss-pots!

Samuel Johnson admirably renders, in his account of Charles, the excitement of the irresistible onward march of Juvenal's Hannibal. Then he adds:

> 'Think nothing gain'd, he cries, till nought remain,
> 'On Moscow's walls till Gothic standards fly,
> 'And all be mine beneath the polar sky.'

This is stately indeed, but the effect of the Latin

> 'acti' inquit 'nihil est, nisi Poeno milite portas
> frangimus et media uexillum pono Subura.'

on me is something like this:

> On Carthaginians! smash the gates! don't mind the
> slaughter!
> The war's not won until I occupy Rome's . . . red-light
> quarter.

Before deciding that this rendering condemns *me*, the reader might consider the next two lines:

> o qualis facies et quali digna tabella,
> cum Gaetula ducem portaret belua luscum!

> What a perfect caricature he would make, the
> one-eyed brass hat on the elephant!

As for the animus, it is perfectly plain in the dismissing couplet:

> i, demens, et saeuas curre per Alpes,
> ut pueris placeas et declamatio fias!

as far removed as possible from Johnson's dignified close:

> He left the name, at which the world grew pale,
> To point a moral, or adorn a tale.

The scholars tell us that the formula *i nunc et* followed by the imperative is used to express derision or remonstrance. With *demens* here there can be no doubt of the contempt: 'Off with you, you crazy fool, scurry over the mountains no civilised person would visit and provide schoolboys with a theme for speech-day exercises!' This is no isolated instance: the same formula is used to pour contempt on handsome young men. Or take this: Johnson attributes to Democritus the talents he himself exhibits in writing the poem:

> Attentive truth and nature to descry,
> And pierce each scene with philosophic eye . . .
> Such was the scorn that fill'd the sage's mind . . .

Juvenal remarks that Democritus merely proves that a genius can be born in a country of fat-heads. Or this: Johnson treats the exploits of Xerxes as a scene of pompous woe. Juvenal attributes the whole story to the Goebbels-like talent of the Greeks for the big historical lie. Or this: when Juvenal introduces a characteristic

Greek type of extreme longevity, he inserts: 'If you can believe anything great Homer says, Nestor must have been the next oldest thing to a crow.' This animus is urbane: but what are we to say when it is turned against life itself? Almost half the poem is a similarly contemptuous account of old age and youth and beauty. Here we are clearly back in the atmosphere of the ninth poem, without the protection of mime, that is, in an atmosphere that repudiates moral concern, and Juvenal has every appearance of enjoying himself: he rollicks and revels in the disgusting and the obscene and displays all his wit.

'Rollicks and revels' may sound like the language of one cock-sure of his thesis and deaf to all other interpretations, so, before illustrating the point as it affects the second half of the poem, let me take an undoubted instance of gratuitous obscenity, obscenity, that is, not required on any theory by the immediate context or the needs of satiric presentation. After saying that the old man is the field for manoeuvres of a whole army of all the known diseases, Juvenal pauses to allow the question: what are the names and number of these diseases? and answers in the well-known literary formula, as we should say, 'ask me rather how many grains of sand there are on the beach'. Ovid used this device to describe the miseries of his exile: 'You could sooner count the thyme of Hybla, the ears of African corn, the birds of the air, the fishes of the sea, the fruits of autumn, the flakes of winter snow.' Juvenal parodies this: 'I could sooner tell you how many adulterers Oppia has had, how many of his patients Dr. Themison murdered in a single autumn, how many partners Basilius defrauded, or how many wards Hirrus.' This is amusing, but Juvenal makes his climax out of a couple of lines I am unable to translate:

> quot longa uiros exorbeat uno
> Maura die, quot discipulos inclinet Amillus.

Now these are two of the sexual abominations which figure in the embroidery of the ninth poem. Surely it could only be before an audience in the mood for Martial's epigrams that these lines would be regarded as a suitable climax?

Once we raise the name of Martial we see that much of the passage on old age is written up from his epigrams or is in his spirit. Thus the minute description of the physical deformities of old age (which may have attracted Hamlet) is in Martial's manner.

One of the jokes, that an old man is so disgusting that he is not only hateful to his wife, children, and himself, but even to the man who hopes to benefit by his will, might have been written by Martial. When we come to the theme of the loss of sexual powers, both the description is like Martial (only more vigorous and outspoken) and the final taunt that there is one form of abomination still open to the old, is a stock joke of Martial's.

That Juvenal takes over the conventional selection of taunts on sexual themes from Martial is even more apparent in the second passage, that on youth and beauty. Here, as in the ninth poem, the note of Martial gains in piquancy by being heard through the solemn orotundities of the epic style. I am sure that much of Juvenal's point in his use of the epic style escapes me. When Juvenal is taking off an extant epic poet, if memory fails, the commentators supply the reference. But Juvenal surely did not confine his parodies to the authors whom chance has allowed to survive to our day? Here is a possible instance from the passage on the physical deformities of old age. Juvenal dwells on the wrinkled hide of the aged and compares it to that of a decayed female monkey's face. The image, I presume, is meant to be precisely disgusting. But in the middle of it Juvenal inserts the fact that the monkey lives 'where Thabraca spreads her shady woods'

umbriferos ubi pandit Thabraca saltus.

The effect on me is not of a windy paraphrase of 'African ape', but of a contrasted natural beauty of woods and of a lovely exotic-sounding proper name: Thabraca. Whatever Juvenal thought of the line itself, in its context it adds to the bite of the following line about the wrinkles on the female monkey's face.

A third strand in Juvenal's wit may be called declamatory, but in a special sense. For the whole passage on youth, as the whole poem, is cast in the form of a declamation. It is also declamatory in spirit. We have been saying just this in pointing to its intellectual feebleness and lack of interest in the truth of what it is talking about. We have been saying this in suggesting that everything is larger than life. Yet although Juvenal's art is at its best in hyperbole, there are special, and inferior, marks of exaggeration which belong (it seems to me) to the Roman *declamatio* proper. Here I regard the wit as excessive or out of place, as temporary or local wit, wit that died the moment it was spoken in the public or

private speech chamber. My first example may seem to be strain-
ing a point, but even so may still stand as indicating the *sort* of
thing I have in mind. The old man gives all his property to Phiale,
who is able to satisfy his indecent demands. Well and good. But
why, I ask, go on to make her, vile as she already is, an old long-
practised inmate of a brothel? The line giving this gratuitous
extra bit of information may be a late addition, but there is no
possibility of removing from the text my second example. After
a long passage on the unhappy end of Priam, Juvenal adds that
this was nothing to what happened to Priam's wife. She unfortu-
nately did not perish with her husband but lived on as a barking
bitch. My third example strikes me as so silly that I wonder
whether Juvenal meant it to be so. He warns parents that if their
sons are handsome they will fall into the clutches of castrators.
Well, it may have had some reference to real life, but surely the
lines: 'no unshapely adolescent was ever castrated in his cruel castle
by a tyrant' belong exclusively to the cloistered world of Roman
declamation?

It is in his treatment of youth and beauty that Juvenal seems
to me to fail most strikingly to hit the classic note. We can find
this note, strange as it may sound, in Yeats. Consider how Juvenal
treats a mother's prayer for her daughter: 'The mother in her eager
fussy worry mixes nonsense in her prayers whenever she sees the
temple of Venus, making a low prayer that her sons may be handsome but openly crying for beauty for her girls. And why not?, she
says. Did not *her* mother rejoice to find Diana fair? Lucretia's fate
should stop such prayers. Virginia would have preferred a humped
back to what happened to her.' Now here is Yeats:

> May she be granted beauty and yet not
> Beauty to make a stranger's eye distraught,
> Or hers before a looking-glass, for such,
> Being made beautiful overmuch,
> Consider beauty a sufficient end,
> Lose natural kindness and maybe
> The heart-revealing intimacy
> That chooses right—and never find a friend.

The full classic note on this commonplace is developed in terms
closer to Juvenal's by Samuel Johnson in his miniature novel,
which might be called *Pride and Prudence*, in which he does full

and final justice to the theme. Here is a synopsis of the plot. The beautiful heroine enters society, enjoys the balls, indulges her powers on her admirers. Well-meaning friends warn her that her beauty is raising powerful enemies against her, but she despises them as strait-laced moralists. Has she not her own sense of honour and knowledge of the world to defend her against all assaults? But those who wish to seduce her mask their approaches: they appeal to her self-interest and flatter her vanity. She falls a victim, loses her social position, and is in every sense ruined. For wit, economy, rapidity, and the George Eliot-like necessity in the tracing out of the consequences of the moral flaw, this 'novel' has no equal:

> Ye nymphs of rosy lips and radiant eyes,
> Whom Pleasure keeps too busy to be wise,
> Whom Joys with soft varieties invite,
> By day the frolick, and the dance by night,
> Who frown with vanity, who smile with art,
> And ask the latest fashion of the heart,
> What care, what rules your heedless charms shall save,
> Each nymph your rival, and each youth your slave?
> Against your fame with fondness hate combines,
> The rival batters, and the lover mines.
> With distant voice neglected Virtue calls,
> Less heard and less, the faint remonstrance falls;
> Tir'd with contempt, she quits the slipp'ry reign,
> And Pride and Prudence take her seat in vain.
> In croud at once, where none the pass defend,
> The harmless Freedom, and the private Friend.
> The guardians yield, by force superior ply'd;
> By Int'rest Prudence; and by Flatt'ry, Pride.
> Now beauty falls betray'd, despis'd, distress'd,
> And hissing Infamy proclaims the rest.

Here we have the profound student of life—and of Boileau:

> Bien-tost dans ce grand Monde, où tu vas l'entraîner,
> Au milieu des écueils qui vont l'environner,
> Crois-tu que toujours ferme aux bords du précipice
> Elle pourra marcher sans que le pié luy glisse?
> Que toujours insensible aux discours enchanteurs
> D'un idolatre amas de jeunes Seducteurs,
> Sa sagesse jamais ne deviendra folie?

D'abord tu la verras, ainsi que dans Clélie,
Recevant ses Amans sous le doux nom d'Amis,
S'en tenir avec eux aux petits soins permis. . . .

But those familiar with the poem will say, there is still *mens
sana* and the philosophic close! Macaulay thought Johnson's final
lines inferior to Juvenal's: 'It must be owned . . . that in the concluding passage the Christian moralist has not made the most of
his advantages, and has fallen decidedly short of the sublimity of
his Pagan model.' Such a remark makes me wonder how closely
Macaulay read his texts. First, if, with Leo, we regard the last two
lines of Juvenal's poem as misplaced, the satire ends with the
reflection that the only sure path to a quiet life is through virtue.
Here I would say that nothing in the poem has prepared us for
and given resonance to this appeal to virtue. Second, the sentence preceding this, defining the choice between virtue and vice,
is not calculated to root our minds in reality: 'Think more highly
of the worries and inhuman labours of Hercules than of Venus,
good dinners, and the feather bed of Sardanapalus.' Third, Juvenal
is sarcastic to the last. This comes out clearly in the context of
mens sana. It can be heard in the preceding line, which is never
quoted with the famous tag:

exta et candiduli diuina tomacula porci.

I therefore take the passage in the spirit of the following: 'You had
better leave prayers to those who know what is good for you. But
if you can't stop yourself asking for something and if you insist
on serving up in your petty temples the inwards and little sausages—
as if that is what gods care for—of a little white porker, well then,
you'd better pray for good sense and good health.' For the truly
classic treatment of the theme we may turn to Ben Jonson:

God wisheth, none should wracke on a strange shelfe:
    To him, man's dearer then t'himselfe,
And, howsoeuer we may thinke things sweet,
    He alwayes giues what he knowes meet;
Which who can vse is happy: Such be thou.
    Thy morning's, and thy euening's vow
Be thankes to him, and earnest prayer, to finde
    A body sound, with sounder minde . . .

Nevertheless, although Juvenal's art does not rest on life-giving 'positives'—if the shorthand will pass—it does not give us the right to proclaim that it rests on 'negatives', despair, disillusion, or hatred of the good. The reason for caution in making such deductions is that one effect of Juvenal's wit is to hold back the question of the reality of what he is handling. Not altogether, of course, for although his wit is exceedingly literary and presupposes knowledge of and critical insight into other kinds of poetry, it is not merely verbal wit. It cannot arise without at least *visual* presentation of the world of things and true reference to the normal movements of the mind in dramatic speech. Yet the effect of being witty about these things is, as it were, to take the 'thinginess' out of things. And a similar argument applies to the effect of the wit on the obscenity: Juvenal's best wit seems to elevate rather than depress the mind.

That this is so may be seen by selecting a single stroke from this poem:

> 'O fortunatam natam me consule Romam!'
> Antoni gladios potuit contemnere si sic
> omnia dixisset.

In what Juvenal calls the divine Second Philippic, the speech (says Mayor) that sealed Cicero's fate, we find Cicero writing, 'I despised the swords of Catiline and shall I tremble at yours, Antony?' But besides securing himself immortality (as the Romans thought) by this work, Cicero had also written a poem extolling his contempt for the swords of Catiline, and so made himself doubly immortal, though this second time, immortally ridiculous, not so much for boasting that he alone had saved Rome, for Juvenal in his eighth poem praises him for that: 'It was Rome not yet enslaved, republican Rome, that gave Cicero the title "Father of his country." but for writing verse with an unfortunate jingle in it. Many writers had made fun of this lapse, but none of their phrases, not even Martial's, can be remembered by heart so easily as Juvenal's epigram: 'He would indeed have had nothing to fear from the swords of Antony if all his writings had been like that one ineffable line.' The brevity of Juvenal and the inevitability of the rhythm raise the point above ordinary sarcasm, so that we think instead of how indeed Cicero had written *omnia*. Thus Juvenal magnifies Cicero by means of a jeer. This, I would remind the beginner, is only one stroke from one poem. Juvenal has many such, for as Boileau truly said:

Ses écrits pleins de feu par tout brillent aux yeux.

I should now like to meet the contention that, if Juvenal was not in earnest about *le coeur humain*, he was passionately concerned with social conditions and in his concern for truth showed a respect for social facts that makes him a reliable 'source' for the historians. Those who hold this view would point to the third poem as indisputable evidence. There, we are told, Juvenal pours out his feelings about the 'big city'; there he is to be compared with the author of the *Apocalypse* declaiming against Babylon; and in rejecting the metropolis Juvenal reveals his own love of the simple life of the small Italian country towns. To this we might add the charge that if the epithet 'stately' does not fit the manner of the tenth poem it is the right word for the third.

Against this I would assert that the theme, or rather, since 'theme' is too grand a word for this poem, the various matters mentioned in it all come under the head of 'selected reasons for finding the life of the Roman *cliens* difficult, daunting, tiresome and uncomfortable'. The poem nowhere makes the slightest pretence to give a picture of Rome from any other point of view. Nor does Juvenal break out of his chosen limits to denounce Rome on general and comprehensive grounds. Nor does he himself say that the life of a client *was* difficult, daunting, tiresome and uncomfortable; he puts into the mouth of a declaimer some of the stock literary jokes about the life of a client and twists them to a pitch of wit they had never received before. Juvenal may in private life have actually thought, on weighing up the pros and cons, that the client's life was intolerable and may even have conjured up a vision of a more satisfactory social system for men in his station, but he does not appear in this rôle in the poem. His attitude towards the subject and the wit he employs make it impossible to guess with any degree of exactitude just how serious conditions in Rome were, either in fact or in Juvenal's estimate. What estimate of the extent of crime can we obtain from this?

> qua fornace graues, qua non incude catenae?
> maximus in uinclis ferri modus, ut timeas ne
> uomer deficiat, ne marra et sarcula desint.

Are we to see Juvenal as 'our industrial correspondent' investigating a 'crisis in metals' and paraphrase like this: 'A visit to our leading blacksmiths in their forges showed them all engaged in turning out massive chains. The manufacture of gyves and fetters now has first priority on our basic iron production so that normal supplies for agricultural implements are seriously threatened.' But if we take it (as we surely must) as hyperbole, can we from the poem determine the exact number of times it is larger than life?

Similarly, it may well be true that Juvenal's heart lay in the smaller Italian towns, but what this poem gives us is once again his love of the sound of proper names. After all, his main point about these towns is that the cost of living in them was much less than in a hovel in Rome. And if we stress the charm of Juvenal's description of a rural open-air peep-show, we should equally note the following:

> uiue bidentis amans et culti uilicus horti,
> unde epulum possis centum dare Pythagoreis.
> est aliquid, quocumque loco, quocumque recessu,
> unius sese dominum fecisse lacertae.

The blatant sarcasm calls for some such rendering as this: 'If you cultivate your love of the spade, Wilkinson, and personally supervise your market garden, you will be able to provide an annual beanfeast for a hundred Pythagoreans (or vegetarians). It is a position of some distinction on the social ladder, however far from the centre of culture you may have to go to achieve it, to call yourself monarch of all not you but a lizard can survey.' This sarcasm is less charming than Martial's humour in 11.18, where, to swell a climax to the charge that his little garden estate is indeed minute, he asserts that there is not even room there for a cucumber to grow straight or for a snake to uncoil.

This third poem of Juvenal's, from the nature of its subject matter, is the one where Martial is most present and is most frequently drawn on. Indeed, so 'stock' and conventional are Juvenal's topics that one of Martial's contemporary British readers could himself have drawn up almost every one of these topics without ever having visited the metropolis. Martial, however, is not only present in the matter, in the selection of aspects for witty development, he is present in the spirit and the tone. This gives me an opportunity to substantiate the claim that Juvenal in his attempt to go 'one better' than Martial extended his efforts to Martial's obscenity. What is to be noted in the example I have chosen is that here Juvenal is under no compulsion from the world of fact.

There is a little scene of ten lines (126–136) where the points are all Martial's. Juvenal has just finished a piece on Greek flatterers as seen by unsuccessful Roman flatterers who find that the Roman is driven out of his occupation by this fierce foreign competition. 'And it is not only foreign competition,' says Juvenal, 'that the poor Roman client has to fear. What chance has the poor man against his richer or nobler fellow-cadger in the race to procure favours from the rich?' Martial in his own person had complained that he and his like were displaced by consuls in their robes of office (10.10) and by senators (12.26). Juvenal was left to make the same joke with the praetor and his lictors. But the financial discrepancy worried them both more than the social: both poets felt more acutely that they were competing as poor men for the dole against the *rich*. On this theme Martial is fond of embroidering the further point (in this resembling some of our later Young Angries) that one of the most galling differences for the poor client between himself and his rich rivals or patrons was in the kind of women each could hire for their pleasure. I forget the exact figure in cash that according to Martial's calculations was the maximum that could be spared from the dole for this essential item of a Roman budget. The point to which I am coming is that in the world of Martial's epigrams this last item *forms the climax* in the list of the poor client's grievances. For instance, in 3.30 Martial asks a doleless client, where now are you going to get the money for your wretched toga (*de rigueur* for social calls on patrons), where's the rent coming from for your windowless garret (Juvenal's *tenebrae*), how are you going to pay the entrance money for the baths, and, lastly, *unde uir es Chiones?* how can you keep up your visits to Snow-white? (This name, it becomes apparent, hides a recognizable person in Martial's world.) Juvenal makes the same point, but with far greater particularity: he *insists* on the obscenity:

The rich man's servant can afford to spend a captain's pay merely for the privilege of one or two 'bouts'—no more—

(*ut semel aut iterum super illam palpitet*: note the prominence of the last insistent word)

with some member of the aristocracy, but if you like the looks of a classy whore, you can only stand and stare, you can't very well afford to invite Snow-white down from her public perch.

I surely do not have to insist that this is not the tone of the author of *Revelations* when his theme is the whore of Babylon. Yet Juvenal couches the point in language as stately as any in the poem:

> et dubitas alta Chionen deducere sella.

The second main characteristic of Juvenal's style, the declamatory note, is perceptible throughout. As in the ninth poem, Juvenal does not take advantage of the dramatic setting in which two old friends are saying good-bye since Umbricius, a native of Rome, is leaving home for ever. Umbricius, however, does not speak to Juvenal, he declaims to the world, and we soon find him addressing a body of 'Quirites', as he takes up his selection of stock topics, only a selection, he says: 'I could add more, but it is time to set out for Cumae.' Yet here as elsewhere the substitution of declamation for drama brings its advantages, since the device enables Juvenal to increase his range of tones beyond those Martial allowed himself in his epigrams. This is clearly to be seen in Juvenal's use of hyperbole. Martial, for instance, in 10.70, where he is giving an account of the way a Roman literary man's day is wasted, slides along pleasantly and the final joke is almost passed off as a fact: 'While it is still dark I make my first morning call on friends who do not return the compliment. Then I go round and call on others—but nobody calls on me. Five hours are wasted in witnessing a will and in paying respects to the consul and the praetor. What a job it is to make my way through the crowds! Often the whole day is wasted listening to a poet recite his verses . . .

> auditur toto saepe poeta die.'

Martial's lines while not imitating talk are close to the spirit of talk, but Juvenal declaims and draws attention to his hyperbole: 'There is no spot on earth however wretched and cut off from civilization that is not preferable to the perpetual dread of fire or falling houses and the thousand and one perils of this inhuman city, where poets continue to recite even in the heat of August.' Once again the final line is sonorous:

et Augusto recitantes mense poetas.

This is not an effect of colloquial speech. It is a device which charges every word almost with a separate point. The total effect, however, is to diminish our concern for the reality of what he is saying. By placing in a scale of dreads, poverty and isolation at the bottom, death in the middle and literary boredom at the climax, we are, it is true, shaken out of our usual responses, and each receives thereby a slight momentary heightening, but, surely, when we settle down, we are left only with the pleasure of verbal play and not with a feeling that the situation is too poignant for any but flippant treatment? In fact by this device we are prevented from gauging how bad Juvenal considered the situation was. A further effect of this type of wit is to rob us of the sense of a governing theme throughout the poem. Our minds stop short at the ironic climax: the theme dissolves into a number of points: points, as it were, that do not join up to make a line, for nothing comes of the point made here. The poets, we find, have put in their last appearance in the poem.

If we nevertheless persist in asking for Juvenal's point of view in the poem, he appears to be playing hide-and-seek with us. For example, if we take the next section of the poem and ask: what does Juvenal feel or wish us to feel about the cult of nymphs and the awe attaching to caves, he seems at first to share Martial's two attitudes. On the one hand, in 10.35, Martial is sly and playful about the relations between King Numa and the nymph Egeria, who used to meet by night in the cave by the spring, on the other, in 4.57, he is willing to accept Nymphs, Nereids, and holy springs, as a 'poetic' amenity of an agreeable holiday resort. Juvenal, as so often, adds to Martial's playfulness the suggestion of a sneer: 'Here where Numa used to "date" his midnight girl friend . . .' and he heightens the contrast between the old religion and present-day Rome by noting (or inventing) the fact that the temple and grove sacred to the Roman Camenae had been hired out to Jews—the very type of professional beggars for Juvenal as for Martial. Juvenal, however, does not lament the passing of the old religion, instead he says: 'how much more vividly we should be aware of the divine spirit of the water if the pool had been kept in its natural state and the surrounding area had not been paved with marble.' The remark of an aesthete, or evidence of a feeling for 'nature'? We cannot tell. All we can say for certain is that the germ of a theme suggested here is not developed: Juvenal does not make it a main charge against Roman life that it is sophisticated or unnatural.

If this is so, we cannot speak of the blend of tones that makes up Juvenal's wit as an *attitude*, for it does not present us with a point of view. Juvenal's wit is often as here merely opportunist: he is out to make any point he can regardless of consistency. This is a serious price to pay for brilliance, for thanks to it Juvenal does not grip his theme, and even if the word 'theme' is confined to each section, he does not bother to bring his points together. For instance, in the well-known passage about the influx of foreigners into Rome, we slide about between remarks that have a whiff of actuality about them and others that are the purest literature. In the same section we have the admirable conciseness of imagery in this line: 'must I give precedence in society to the man carried to Rome on the wind that brings us the plum and the fig?'

aduectus Romam quo pruna et cottana uento.

On the other hand, after summing up the passage on the versatility of the Greek on the make by saying: 'and bid him fly into the sky, he'll do it', Juvenal adds: 'no exaggeration, you know; it wasn't a Moor, a Sarmatian or a Thracian who was the first pioneer aeronaut, but a true-born Athenian' and on the instant we feel that this is one more of the stock topics of the declaimer.

In fact once the unreality sets in we soon find ourselves back in the atmosphere of the ninth poem and of Martial's obscenity, as in the following epigram (4.5): 'You are a good fellow and you have no fortune: you say only what your heart prompts. What's your object in coming to Rome, then, Fabianus? You have no reputation as a go-between or as a good man to have at a drunken party . . . you wouldn't be able to seduce your best friend's wife or rise to the demands of passion-freezing old hags . . .' which, I take it, gave Juvenal the suggestion for: 'The Greek will not stop at seducing your wife, deflowering your daughter, her fiancé, your son, and, if none of these opportunities offers, he will go for his best friend's grandmother.' With the substitution of one more of Juvenal's clever dirty words for the consecrated obscenity of Martial (*resupinare* for *arrigere*) we have an identical attitude. Umbricius may be giving us a Roman, but surely not a noble Roman attitude.

There is, however, one passage in the poem not open to the charge of unreality. I believe that when Martial and Juvenal complain of the cost of living they are not merely exploiting a stock topic but are adding something from their own stock of feeling. Here Juvenal's declamatory manner gives point to what may well be genuine indignation and resentment. Here at any rate it is noteworthy that the movement of Juvenal's mind is reversed: he goes from literature and 'commonplaces' to particularities. The two styles are in pointed contrast. First, Juvenal prepares a stroke of his finest wit. As the stroke is going to depend on the sanctity of oaths, he speaks first of the most reverend figures of Roman religion. He even invokes the gods of Greece before whom perjury was unthinkable. Then he says: 'even if you pronounce the most solemn oath nobody will believe you if you are poor. The poor have nothing to fear from the vengeance of the gods—why, when they defy the gods they are sure of pardon, for in the eyes of the gods a poor man is not regarded as a real person to be taken seriously any more than he is so considered by the rich.' All this is put into nine words by Juvenal:

> contemnere fulmina pauper
> creditur atque deos dis ignoscentibus ipsis.

After this hyperbole Juvenal switches us with a jolt to earth and the actual state of Martial and himself, to the difficulty of paying for a toga, the cost of keeping it white, the price of decent shoes, and the subterfuges needed to hide either repair or want of repair. And if there is a *cri de coeur* in Juvenal, it is surely (*pace* Marmorale) in these lines:

> nil habet infelix paupertas durius in se
> quam quod ridiculos homines facit.

Here Naevolus and Umbricius, Juvenal and Martial, speak in unison. *Paupertas*, as the ninth poem showed, is the state of a man with several servants and perhaps a small farm as well as a garret in the city. It is anything short of wealth and an assured position. *Infelix* means among other things that you can't secure one of the plums the rich have it in their power to distribute. It also suggests that the distribution of these plums is as capricious as fortune itself. When men have made this complaint in modern times the consequence has sometimes been social revolution. Juvenal makes the suggestion only to turn it into a bitter joke: 'The poor of Rome should acquire the military virtues of the ancient *plebs* in their struggle against the patricians and leave the city in a body until they can get better terms.' But for Juvenal as for Martial the real sting lies in *ridiculos*. Their problem was how to avoid the jokes and jibes of society, how to get on the side of the laughers, how to avoid becoming their butt. Their solution of the problem was either to cadge a sufficiency or to go where the cost of living was lower. The latter was Umbricius' plan, and Juvenal's drift culminates in the complaint that everything in Rome costs money, even to gain admittance to our patrons; even sleep costs money, for only those with a *rus in urbe* can get far enough away from the noise of the streets.

The temptation to see Juvenal as a true reporter of *other* features of Roman life than those affecting the cost of living of the respectable poor is greatest in the second half of the poem, where the tone is lighter and where comment gives way to description. For many readers the little pictures in this part of the poem are the most delightful things in Juvenal. The temptation to believe that these pictures are addressed exclusively to the eye is increased by little natural touches, such as the description of the poor man's garret at the top of the tenement, where cooing doves lay their eggs on the roof. Nevertheless, as with the passage already discussed about Sejanus, so here we should not be misled into reading each pictorial section as mere description. *They are vehicles of wit* and they are heightened for the sake of the wit. For example, the climax of the description of the poor man's library is the one word which conveys the thought that the mice eat his Greek manuscripts through pure ignorance of the precious language. The contrasting section on the profitable fire in the rich man's house is an expansion of one of Martial's epigrams. In the piece about the crowds of clients on their way to their patrons, it is doubtful whether in fact because of the slow progress of these clients towards their free meal or the dole they had to bring enormous perambulating kitchens along with them and eat on the way. And surely the tone of voice when speaking of the danger from heavy traffic should put us on the alert not to overdo our efforts to treat as photographic the impression Juvenal gives us here of an actual street sight. For after all, it leads up to a piece of mock epic where the crushed man's soul is stuck on the banks of the Styx without a penny while his servants are expecting him home for dinner. Similarly, the tone of the passage about the drunken bully is such as to preclude our thinking that the description is of facts.

These temptations proved too strong for those who from Boileau onwards have tried to give the spirit of the poem by transferring the scene to their own capitals. Because they yield to these temptations, their versions have very little to offer us of Juvenal's spirit. They have the further defect of their method in that Juvenal's Rome differs from any modern Babylon. Although in our modern capitals we hear of appalling examples of vice and of human beings reduced to extreme degradation, yet in the narrow segment of society corresponding to that Juvenal is concerned with, it would be ludicrous and not witty to present a proud and decent 'intellectual' claiming merit for being unable to lie with his best friend's grandmother. But once you substitute something like this:

> J'ignore ce grand art qui gagne une maîtresse

we can hardly expect to find much of Juvenal in the French. And once you make such changes in the spirit, the point of retaining Juvenal's external framework goes.

Dryden, surprisingly, yields very little to the amateur who tries to feel his way into Juvenal's poem by reading his version. As a matter of fact the spirit of Juvenal, as van Doren pointed out, is to be found rather in his portrait of Zimri than in his translation of the passage about the supple Greek. Compare, for instance, this from the translation:

> Quick Witted, Brazen-fac'd, with fluent Tongues,
> Patient of Labours, and dissembling Wrongs,
> Riddle me this, and guess him if you can,
> Who bears a Nation in a single Man?
> A Cook, a Conjuror, a Rhetorician,
> A Painter, Pedant, a Geometrician,
> A Dancer on the Ropes, and a Physician . . .

> The Nation is compos'd of such as these.
> All *Greece* is one Commedian . . .

with this:

> A man so various, that he seem'd to be
> Not one, but all Mankind's Epitome.
> Stiff in Opinions, always in the wrong;
> Was Everything by starts, and Nothing long:
> But, in the course of one revolving Moon,
> Was Chymist, Fidler, States-man, and Buffoon;
> Then all for Women, Painting, Rhiming, Drinking,
> Besides ten thousand Freaks that died in thinking.

But for my argument these modern versions of Juvenal have a value in that by their failures they support my two negative contentions that Juvenal's is not a topical poem written with an eye on actual conditions and it does not exhibit moral earnestness. It is hardly an exaggeration to say the comparative failure of Johnson's *London* is due to the error of giving the poem topical point and substituting a grave and weighty moral tone for the varied but never consistent wit of Juvenal. Certainly, the very possibility of matching Juvenal's range of tone was lost once Johnson had decided to draw on Boileau for the rugged and surly Thales:

> Je suis rustique et fier, et j'ai l'âme grossière

and on Oldham for the 'patriotic' appeals to pre-Conquest or Plantagenet England. Boileau, indeed, who had in addition made his retiring Parisian a poet, found it impossible to maintain the tone of proud dignity throughout and split up his original satire into two. The first is 'noble', the sixth, as it now stands, is 'comic'.

That Johnson's attempt to maintain one tone throughout does put a strain on the poem we may see by contrasting passages from the two halves. For instance,

> Turn from the glitt'ring bribe thy scornful eye,
> Nor sell for gold, what gold could never buy,
> The peaceful slumber, self-approving day,
> Unsullied fame, and conscience ever gay . . .

and

> Scarce can our fields, such crowds at Tyburn die,
> With hemp the gallows and the fleet supply . . .

or

> Orgilio sees the golden pile aspire,
> And hopes from angry heav'n another fire . . .

Johnson's wit does not correspond to a twinkle in the eye: it does not invite the reader to take everything with a pinch of salt. On the contrary, it forces the reader, first, to consider the truth of the apparent statement, and when, after consideration, we find truth wanting, we are struck all the more with the unreality of the verse.

Yet there is at least one passage where Johnson, while leaving what we may call social or moral reality, has succeeding in creating something that by contrast might be called purely poetic reality. Many people have thought that in this passage he rivals or surpasses Juvenal. The facts underlying what is perhaps not well conveyed by this awkward critical terminology can be brought out by considering the raw material, as it were, that Johnson worked on and worked up into this 'pure' poetry: for I think it will be admitted that the following lines have a good *prima facie* claim to be Johnson's starting point:

> If this you 'scape, twenty to one, you meet
> Some of the drunken Scowrers of the Street,
> Flush'd with success of warlike Deeds perform'd,
> Of Constables subdu'd, and Brothels storm'd;
> These, if a Quarrel, or a Fray be mist,
> Are ill at ease a nights, and want their Rest.
> For mischief is a Lechery to some,
> And serves to make them sleep like *Laudanum*.
> Yet heated, as they are, with Youth and Wine,
> If they discern a train of Flambeaus shine,
> If a Great Man with his gilt Coach appear,
> And a strong Guard of Foot-boys in the rere,
> The Rascals sneak, and shrink their Heads for fear.

Oldham brought an active, poetic brain to the reading of Juvenal, and drew on his own experience. The drunken scourers of the London streets were a topical social fact, and they are present as such in this passage, though the bullies also faintly recall the sons of Belial. But if the strength of the passage lies in its ability to refer us to appropriate objects, its weakness is undoubtedly its diffuseness. Johnson not only concentrates and reinforces the points; by removing the topicality of particular reference, he achieves the 'concrete abstract' to perfection:

> Some fiery fop, with new commission vain,
> Who sleeps on brambles till he kills his man;
> Some frolick drunkard, reeling from a feast,
> Provokes a broil, and stabs you for a jest.
> Yet ev'n these heroes, mischievously gay,
> Lords of the street, and terrors of the way;
> Flush'd as they are with folly, youth and wine,
> Their prudent insults to the poor confine;
> Afar they mark the flambeau's bright approach,
> And shun the shining train, and golden coach.

This passage, however, marks an exception, and diverts us from the general impression that Johnson is narrower in range than Juvenal. Another narrowing factor has often been pointed out, and I refer to it here only to bring out the contrasting felicity of Juvenal in a respect where I may have appeared till now excessively grudging. Critics have often remarked that Johnson has made his Thales seem to be heading for a never-never land, and certainly from his expressions about his destination on leaving London, the reader might retort that he was living in a fool's paradise if he supposed he could find anything so vaguely idyllic as

> Some pleasing bank where verdant osiers play,
> Some peaceful vale with nature's paintings gay . . .

This weak form of generality reveals how small Johnson's interest in the theme must have been. It enables me to say that in contrast with this Juvenal's references to the countryside are concrete!

The want of help from our own poets is felt the more acutely since the whole interpretation of Juvenal's poem depends on how we take the ground tone, which is indeed a solemn and sonorous hexameter—though solemn, as we have seen, only in the roll and rhythm of the words. The perpetual return to a line such as this:

> fixa catenatae siluit compago tabernae

(even though here Juvenal may be evoking the noise of the locking up) does not bear on the surface the reason why it is so and not otherwise. If there is no wit in so casting the poem, then the verdict on it as a whole must be: it is an exhibition piece. The enormous energy put out to carry off the variety of approaches— for each single section is built up in a different way—commands

respect. It is possible to read the poem as a straight piece of declamation, and so many of the external features of declamation are
fully employed that we might say that in addition to Martial the
contemporary English reader would have required every chapter
of a handbook on declamation to appreciate the poem. Yet if it is
merely a wonderful exhibition piece, my respect is cool. I am
inclined to suspect and certainly to hope that there is a special
point in the external structure and the general tone: that, in a
word, Umbricius is not Martial, but Juvenal himself recalling in
verse the recitations he had so often delivered in prose and laughing both at himself in that rôle and at the attempt by contemporary writers of solemn hexameters to take themselves seriously.
The poem in that case would be a genuine and witty drama and
a piece of literary not social criticism.

To get the greatest pleasure from Juvenal one should see that
his art is at its characteristic best when it stands some way off
from ordinary reality. The pleasure reaches its height when the
distance is neither too great nor too small. For if Juvenal abandons reality altogether we get merely verbal points, points which
may amuse us for a second or two but never anchor themselves
in the mind. The delightful wit in Juvenal differs from merely
verbal wit very much as Marvell's 'green thought' differs from
the Antipodes who walk with their heads. I take this analogy
from James Smith, who rightly pointed out that the elements in
the latter conceit 'come together only for a moment, at that
moment cause surprise and perhaps pleasure, and then immediately
fly apart' whereas in the former the figure once made does not
disintegrate: 'it offers something unified and "solid" for our
contemplation which, the longer we contemplate, only grows the
more solid'.

The general misunderstanding of Juvenal (as it seems to me)
arises because to create his own poetic reality he has borrowed
from ordinary life topics and situations that provoke powerful
feelings. But his 'world' is as remote from ours as that of T. F.
Powys from the Christian conception. To pursue this argument
and to reveal the heights to which Juvenal can carry us if we will
only follow as he guides and take him as he wanted to be taken,
I must now tackle the sixth and by far the longest poem in the

collection. Since my essay is only an introduction to and not a study of Juvenal, I cannot hope to consider this poem as a whole. All that I can manage is to indicate in a general way how to take it and to fasten on one or two passages where Juvenal exhibits his art at its best.

What has chiefly hindered the true appreciation of this poem is a mistaken notion about its temperature. Many critics have supposed that it came, as we say, straight from the heart, and that it is the immediate result of indulging in neurotic feelings about women. The more absurd of these critics have claimed on the strength of this poem that Juvenal must have suffered in his own person at the hands of one or more women and in consequence taken to homosexuality! Against this I would say that the last thing we should be thinking of if we are trying to feel and enjoy Juvenal's poetry as deeply as ever we can is the presence of a *personal* animus against one woman or one class of women. The poem can never be presented as the supreme *pièce justificative* when asking whether Juvenal is a classic as long as we are reading it as the outpourings of a frustrated neurotic. When Dryden wrote that 'the whole World must allow this to be the wittiest of his Satyrs' and Boileau named it 'son plus bel ouvrage', they were surely taking the poem as something other than a purely personal effusion.

If the opening lines may be taken as a fair place to give us the clue to the tone of the poem, the reader will be bound to concede that here Juvenal is handling a commonplace. The reference to Cynthia suggests that Juvenal wished us to recall how Propertius had handled this commonplace. The beginner curious to see how Juvenal improves on his predecessors may be glad to have this specimen:

> qui quaerit Tatios ueteres durasque Sabinas,
>   hic posuit nostra nuper in urbe pedem.
> tu prius et fluctus poteris siccare marinos,
>   altaque mortali deripere astra manu,
> quam facere ut nostrae nolint peccare puellae:
>   hic mos Saturno regna tenente fuit,
> et cum Deucalionis aquae fluxere per orbem
>   et post antiquas Deucalionis aquas . . .

which may be paraphrased as: 'After a very short time in the city the stranger gives up the search for good old-fashioned Romans.

It would be easier to dry up the ocean or pull down the stars than to try by mere human agency to stop our girls from misbehaving. This was not even possible when Saturn was in power or at the time of the flood and at no time since the flood subsided—and that was long ago.'

The point of the opening may also have been to reply to something in Martial. Martial's sixth book opens with a series of epigrams written to curry favour with Domitian. One of the subjects that recur there (and elsewhere) is praise of the Emperor for reviving the Julian law against adultery. We know that Juvenal had at least one of these epigrams in mind, for he uses a point from (6.7): 'A little month, nay not so much, has passed since the law against adultery ordered Fidelity (*Pudicitia*) to come back to the homes of married people, yet in that time Telesilla has outdone those who make a profession of adultery. She has changed husbands ten times and thus become a sort of legal law-breaker':

> quae nubit totiens, non nubit: adultera lege est.

Juvenal gave his representative of the type eight husbands in five autumns. And just before this Martial addressed the Emperor somewhat as follows (6.4): 'Almighty moral censor, king of kings, what Rome owes to you! What triumphs, what new churches and old ones rebuilding, what public shows! So many new gods, so many new cities added! Yet more than all these, Rome owes it to you that she is chaste (*pudica*)!'

Credo, Juvenal begins and gives us irony in his best vein on this theme of Fidelity (*Pudicitia*). It is as if he were making a satirical re-hash of the wonderful fifth book of Lucretius, where the progress of man is sketched stage by stage from the earliest days to the advent of civilization. But Juvenal has no reverence for his Adam and Eve: hairy woman and acorn-belching man. Yet, he says, as long as Jupiter was too young to covet the daughters of earth, none of these people thought of adultery. Here again Juvenal goes beyond Martial, who had written (6.2): 'Before you re-enacted the laws against sexual crimes, o Caesar, it was a regular sport to break the laws of wedlock with its sacred torch. . . .'. Contrast Juvenal: 'It is a custom of the most authentic antiquity, o Posthumus, to rattle the springs of another man's marriage bed in contempt of the sacred godhead forced to look down on you in the act. . . .'. The commentators here rightly remind us of Naevolus, who proved his adultery by the creaking of the other man's marriage bed.

How then are we to take this opening? Surely in the spirit of Boileau's *Satire X*, where he opens in imitation of Juvenal by rallying a polite court rake on his desire to get married, but allows the would-be husband the following reply:

> Charmé de Juvenal, et plein de son esprit,
> Venez-vous, diras-tu, dans une piece outrée,
> Comme luy nous chanter: Que dès le tempts de Rhée
> La Chasteté déja, la rougeur sur le front,
> Avoit chés les Humains receu plus d'un affront:
> Qu'on vit avec le fer naistre les Injustices,
> L'Impieté, l'Orgueil, et tous les autres Vices,
> Mais que la Bonne foy dans l'amour conjugal
> N'alla point jusqu'au temps du troisième Métal?
> Ces mots ont dans sa bouche une emphâze admirable:

Precisely: the pleasure we get from the opening of his poem is derived in part from its airy disdain of common sense or earnestness. We do not need Alcippe to remind us that this is not a sober argument.

Juvenal guides us at once into the regular path of the declamation:

> ferre potes dominam saluis tot restibus ullam?

(which reminds us again of the *saluis his collibus* of the ninth poem) and he crowns the section with a piece of hyperbole: if death is not preferable to marriage, why not choose as the partner of your bed a pliant and peaceable youth? Surely it is not merely snobbish to call provincial the man who would direct us at this moment to consider whether Juvenal is not being all-too-autobiographical here? Surely the note of the well-bred man is rather this of Ruperti's (whom I here take the opportunity of recommending as far and away the best guide to Juvenal's meaning for those with a 'gentleman's'—of the old school—knowledge of Latin. He was once highly esteemed in England, and it is a pleasure to find scholars again remembering him, Jachmann, notably, and W. C. Helmbold, who writes of Mayor's impudence and Housman's coldness towards Ruperti):

Hanc autem non veram poetae mentem esse, sed salse potius et scoptice notari Postumum, *notissimum moechorum* (v. 42) quilibet vel me non monente intelliget.

Surely it is clear that we are in the world of Martial and the ninth poem? Ursidius approves of the Julian law and like Naevolus, who was, we recall, *notior Aufidio moechus*, is called on to explain the change in his *propositum uitae.*

That the ninth poem is relevant here we are again reminded by the reference to the mime. Juvenal says in effect: 'Nothing is impossible if Ursidius submits to monogamy; if he who used to be notorious for his adventures with married women like a fool puts his face between the shafts when he had so often played the part of Latinus hiding in a basket like some Falstaff in fear of discovery by the enraged husband.' Juvenal intensifies the wit step by step. The rake wants a good old-fashioned wife, as if he did not know from Martial the vices of girls who have not yet lost their virginity! As if one husband could be enough for any woman! There may be more likelihood of finding a chaste woman in one of the small Italian country towns, yet who can guarantee that there are no modern Didos even in the remote Hebrides or that Jupiter and Mars have lost their zest for roving expeditions in the virgin wilds?

From the mime it was an easy transition to the stage, and from the lonely countryside it was an easy contrast to move to the crowded theatre. At the same time Juvenal pushes to the extreme the theme of female lubricity—again by reference to the actress in the mime who played 'opposite' Latinus. But if, as it were, Juvenal starts at the bottom again on the subject of female infatuation with actors, he soon mounts with the help of Martial to the final point of the section: 'Go through with all the pomp of a rich and fashionable marriage and you will find in the expensive aristocratic cot that you have acquired a gladiator's bastard for a legal heir.'

So far the poem has gone swinging forward without a break, keeping to the light, scornful, mocking note set at the opening, but gaining point, perhaps, in the last section from the use of proper names, for I assume that when, for instance, Juvenal contrasts the popularity of actors and musicians in upper-class female society with the absurdity of supposing that *ces dames* could fall in love with a university professor, he was referring to the famous

Quintilian, who may have been his own professor. If so, it would be out of keeping if the other names were merely generic. Now, however, the style changes to permit Juvenal to make two portraits. Both are conceived in the hyperbolic mode beloved of the rhetoricians: everything is exaggerated and the contrasts are extreme, the emphasis loud and obvious. Though not to my taste, they are broadly grounded on common facts of nature, but they add nothing to the facts. As elsewhere, though, they are not mere portraits but vehicles of wit. The—if I may be permitted the joke —levanting senator's wife is bad enough to give even the lurid East a shock. I feel that Juvenal is here introducing the mock epic note: 'forgetful she of home and husband and her blood, deaf to the claims of country and her weeping children' in order to introduce bathos: 'and what will astonish you more, able to do without the theatre and Paris' (the dancer, of course.) The style leads to and favours mere point, dear to the Romans, but not to me, for instance: 'she defied the ocean, having long ago treated her good name in the same way' and to the sort of 'sentence' dear to the Middle Ages: 'The most timorous of women is brave when courage is needed . . . for crime . . .' though, in defence of Juvenal it must be said that his language responds to the demands of this style:

> quae moechum sequitur stomacho ualet.

And there is even a ghastly humour—the line continues:

> illa maritum
> conuomit . . .

Especially when the noble lady calls her broken-down gladiator Sergiolus, we hardly need the lower Sunday papers to bring to mind modern parallels. So far, then, we have not come across a tone in the poem which sends us back either to the author's private life or to *serious* thoughts about Roman scandals.

To cap this first portrait, Juvenal makes an even heavier borrowing from the rhetoricians, who had a ghoulish interest in imagining fictitious law cases in which the kind of situation we are more familiar with from Marina in the brothel in *Pericles* was described in loving detail. Juvenal adapts this material to fit the case of Messalina. This section has always been admired: I therefore regret that I cannot speak of it with much warmth, for it is too external to be powerful. Juvenal has not put much into it; he has relied on the brute facts—summed up in the contrast *meretrix Augusta*—to do all the work for him.

So much I hope will serve to give a general impression of Juvenal's manner in this poem. To appreciate his art we must come closer to the text. Here the amateur begins to feel the weakness of his status. On every page of this essay I can't help imagining the comment of some younger student of English, perhaps not very well acquainted either with Latin literature or the way in which it is taught. At my elbow I hear him saying with a friendly sneer: 'you may have been able to suggest to those who know only Latin reasons for taking up Dryden or Johnson, but to *us* your attempts to come close to the Latin text appear surprisingly . . . timid. We are used to something more *serré*: you don't disentangle the imagery or go into detail about the movement, in fact you can't be said to have *analyzed* the poetry at all.' In my defence I must plead that if I tried any such thing I should very soon find myself *au bout de mon latin*. It is for the expert to say how much farther in this direction he can go without feeling insecure.

Here, then, with all reserves, is my first specimen:

'Nullane de tantis gregibus tibi digna uidetur?'
sit formonsa decens diues fecunda, uetustos
porticibus disponat auos, intactior omni
crinibus effusis bellum dirimente Sabina,
rara auis in terris nigroque simillima cycno:
quis feret uxorem cui constant omnia? malo,
malo Venustinam quam te, Cornelia mater
Gracchorum, si cum magnis uirtutibus adfers
grande supercilium et numeras in dote triumphos.
tolle tuum, precor, Hannibalem uictumque Syphacem
in castris, et cum tota Carthagine migra!
'parce, precor, Paean, et tu, dea, pone sagittas:
nil pueri faciunt, ipsam configite matrem!'
Amphion clamat; sed Paean contrahit arcum.
extulit ergo greges natorum ipsumque parentem,
dum sibi nobilior Latonae gente uidetur
atque eadem scrofa Niobe fecundior alba.
quae tanti grauitas, quae forma, ut se tibi semper
inputet? huius enim rari summique uoluptas
nulla boni, quotiens animo corrupta superbo

plus aloes quam mellis habet. quis deditus autem
usque adeo est, ut non illam quam laudibus effert
horreat inque diem septenis oderit horis?

(6.161–183)

The point I wish to illustrate is Juvenal's rapidity and brevity.
I do not know what in

sit formonsa decens diues fecunda

decens adds to *formonsa*, but as the dictionary quotes from Suetonius *pulcher et decens*, I suppose that the general impression of
a rapid summary of the points that would recommend a wife
would not be broken for a Roman reader;

uetustos
porticibus disponat auos

is admirable pictorial shorthand for the titled lady who brings in
her trousseau and starts furnishing the marital home with the
battered busts of her heroic forbears;

omni intactior
crinibus effusis bellum dirimente Sabina

is a vivid compression of Livy's famous account of the Rape, and
reinforces the moral aspect of having blue blood, while the wit of

quis feret uxorem cui constant omnia?

is well prepared for by the two proverbial phrases:

rara auis in terris nigroque simillima cycno.

But now Juvenal moves forward to a fresh point: not the virtues themselves are nauseous but the pride that accompanies
them. Out of the 'ancestral portraits' image comes, first,

Cornelia mater
Gracchorum

but the full force of the image, anticipated in my comment above,
comes out in this: 'rather, much rather a poor and lowly creature
than you, Cornelia, if your lofty qualities are matched by your
hauteur and you count the military honours in your family as part
of the cash value of your dowry.' (Here, to anticipate a discussion

to come later on, we may glance at the ninth poem, where
Naevolus asks for *his* triumphs to be given their true cash value:
compare here

> numeras in dote triumphos

and there

> numerentur deinde labores.)

Now, as the second and most surprising development of the
image, Juvenal asks for immediate divorce—politely, unlike the
husband of the beauty on the decline, who left it to his secretary
to tell his wife to pack up her knicknacks and be off—'please cart
away the honourable mentions of your ancestors' victories over
Hannibal, etc.'

> et cum tota Carthagine migra!

Is there anything here that suggests pressure from painful personal memories? Boileau at least was glad to borrow this passage:

> Si quelque objet pareil chez moy, deçà les Monts,
> Pour m'épouser entroit avec tous ces grands noms,
> Le sourcil rehaussé d'orgueilleuses chimeres,
> Je lui dirois bien-tost: 'Je connois tous vos Peres:
> Je sçay qu'ils ont brillé dans ce fameux combat
> Où sous l'un des Valois Enguien sauva l'Etat.
> D'Hozier n'en convient pas: mais, quoy qu'il en
> puisse estre:
> Je ne suis point si sot que d'épouser mon maistre.
> Ainsi donc au plûtost délogeant de ces lieux,
> Allez, Princesse, allez avec tous vos Ayeux
> Coucher, si vous voulez, aux champs de Cerizoles.
> Ma maison, ni mon lit ne sont point faits pour vous.'

This comparison will I hope bring out the economy of Juvenal
and the superior force and concreteness of his imagery, for the
want of which Boileau seems over-explicit, too explanatory.

The comparison also brings out the greater seriousness of Juvenal's feeling. Boileau, after all, is merely giving us an amusing
trait d'esprit: Juvenal's hyperbole contains a weightier point. But
before exploding it he introduces an image that expands the
theme. When we hear the first line: 'Mercy, I beg, Apollo, and
you, Goddess, lay down your bow' we do not at once recall
Niobe's monstrous pride in her fecundity: we seem to be preci-
pitated into something new and are left to ourselves to make the

connection with what has gone before. And after Juvenal has deployed his sarcasm over the legendary figure, we are again surprised to find that he has poured it out in order to concentrate his feeling against his original object. Niobe's husband is made to appeal to Apollo to direct his shafts against the proper target: 'shoot down their mother, not my innocent boys.' But Apollo fires both at them and him and Niobe has to conduct a mass funeral. So numerous were her offspring that instead of comparing herself to the mother of Apollo and Diana she should more appropriately have challenged the famous white sow which littered thirty little pigs on the hill where Lavinium was founded, as Virgil had reported (as Juvenal recalled in 12.72–74):

> sublimis apex, cui candida nomen
> scrofa dedit, laetis Phrygibus mirabile sumen,
> et numquam uisis triginta clara mamillis.

The feeling against the proud aristocrat has thus gained in volume by this apparent digression, as we see when Juvenal returns to the charge. No Roman virtue or beauty, he says, is tolerable if it is made a commercial score against you. The force of *inputet* is not quite clear to me, but it is used in a similar context in the fifth poem, where the rich man destroys the virtue of his invitation by scoring it against the poor man. Juvenal then concludes: even the greatest love is poisoned by such calculating pride, which from causing a shudder in the lover turns love into hate for the greater part of each working day.

Though the passage exhibits Juvenal's art at its best, the development of thought and feeling through hyperbole to a *serious* conclusion is slight. For its fuller development we must turn to the end of the poem, where Juvenal traces the connections between female depravity and the love of the occult, the theme so often handled by Mr. Eliot, in *Sweeney Agonistes*, for instance, and in *The Waste Land*, and, generalised, in *The Dry Salvages*:

> To communicate with Mars, converse with spirits,
> To report the behaviour of the sea monster,
> Describe the horoscope, haruspicate or scry,
> Observe disease in signatures, evoke
> Biography from the wrinkles of the palm
> And tragedy from fingers; release omens
> By sortilege, or tea leaves, riddle the inevitable

> With playing cards, fiddle with pentagrams
> Or barbituric acids, or dissect
> The recurrent image into pre-conscious terrors—
> To explore the womb, or tomb, or dreams; all these
>   are usual
> Pastimes and drugs, and features of the press:
> And always will be, some of them especially
> When there is distress of nations and perplexity
> Whether on the shores of Asia, or in the Edgware Road.

It will be helpful to keep this passage in mind, if only to prevent us from seeing the manifestations of Roman superstition as something too remote, too unlike our own experience. For though Juvenal's way is to throw into prominence the fantastic side of the various kinds of traffic with the unseen, his ultimate object is a truth.

The *finale* begins with dramatic suddenness at the end of line 511—though it may have had an introduction now lost. As it stands, it begins with *ecce* and the sudden entrance into the arena, as it were, of a chorus of squeaking eunuchs, who make way for their leader, a huge Archigallus, Bellona's bridegroom indeed, but bridegroom of a Bellona affiliated to the Great Mother, and therefore a eunuch by his own act. Juvenal presents him as at once formidable, awe-inspiring and ridiculous; *grande sonat* in the epic style, but only to prophesy the obvious—that September in Rome is a dangerous month (remember Dr. Themison!)—and to perform the ritual purification for a year's sins by causing them to pass into the lady's cast-off clothes, which he gratefully receives for the purpose.

The commentators are always pointing out how little interest Juvenal had in providing elegant transitions from one part of his poem to the next, and there is no doubt that Juvenal, unlike Boileau and Pope, usually does not seem to have felt himself obliged to hide the fact that there was no other continuity than the shock of change in passing from one section to another. It is therefore noteworthy that the next section—on Oriental religion—is tightly organized and glides imperceptibly into the following topic—soothsayers—in a way unmatched in the rest of Juvenal's poems. This exceptional attention to surface neatness makes his connecting thought clear. Juvenal advances his theme by, roughly speaking, contrasting this passive and painless vicarious expiation by one woman with the extremely painful lengths another will go to when so commanded by Isis. What a travesty of the idea of the divine!

> en animam et mentem cum qua di nocte loquantur!

Juvenal even supposes that the priest who impersonates Anubis sneers under his mask at the adoring mob at his heels. The tone of sarcasm comes out strongly when women in tears ask pardon for the sin of sleeping with their husbands, as it were, in Lent—a terrible crime demanding terrible expiation; nothing less than a huge goose and a little cake will suffice to bribe Osiris into giving absolution. The sarcasm is increased as Juvenal turns to the religion of the Jews, for here women get whatever they want on the cheapest terms, and all their dreams interpreted by one who is in direct touch with the All-High. Yet the sarcasm is clearly directed at those who could believe such a claim, and at the effrontery of women in putting religion to the service of their amorous longings.

I shall not follow Juvenal throughout the section but leap forward to the first major transition, from the superstitious belief in fortune-telling to the traffic in drugs, magic and poison. The first step is masterly: we take leave of a poor woman consulting on the racecourse whether to desert her small innkeeper husband or lover and marry the man who sells military cloaks:

> an saga uendenti nubat caupone relicto.

This provides Juvenal with the perfect springboard: at least the poor woman looks forward to becoming a mother at whatever cost to her attractiveness. She does not use drugs to procure abortion.

We now catch Juvenal improving on himself. In his third poem he had touched on the theme of the substitution of *nouveaux-riches* outsiders for Romans in the giving of gladiatorial shows:

> inde reuersi
> conducunt foricas, et cur non omnia? cum sint
> quales ex humili magna ad fastigia rerum
> extollit quotiens uoluit Fortuna iocari.

> From thence return'd, their sordid Avarice rakes
> In Excrements again, and hires the Jakes.
> Why hire they not the Town, not ev'ry thing,

Since such as they have Fortune in a String?
Who, for her pleasure, can her Fools advance;
And toss 'em topmost on the Wheel of Chance.

In the sixth poem we are given dramatically what in the third poem is merely stated. It is a scene worthy of Dickens or Victor Hugo. The scene, as I imagine it, would be a *cloaca*: it is night: here come women anxious to get rid of their new-born children, and here, too, come others eager to fill an empty cradle, particularly the wilfully sterile ladies of the best families whose 'finds' will be destined to fill the highest positions in Church and State: and looking on the scene, smiling on the naked babies, stands the goddess Fortuna and takes the lucky ones up and wraps them carefully in her cloak. She herself offers them to the aristocratic 'mothers' and she enjoys the private farce or mime she is preparing for herself—for she will follow the careers of the foundlings until they in fact reach the highest positions.

With wonderful command of tone Juvenal switches us from this larger-than-life scene to the neat, clipped irony of the following:

The craving Wife the force of Magick tries,
And Philters for th'unable Husband buys:
The Potion works not on the part design'd;
But turns his Brain, and stupifies his Mind.

But Dryden has missed the felicity of Juvenal's brevity, as here:

et solea pulsare natis: quod desipis, inde est,
inde animi caligo et magna obliuio rerum
quas modo gessisti.

In this section there is far greater play of mind than in the following from Tennyson:

Lucilia, wedded to Lucretius, found
Her master cold . . .
She brook'd it not; but wrathful, petulant,
Dreaming some rival, sought and found a witch
Who brew'd the philtre which had power, they said,
To lead an errant passion home again.
And this, at times, she mingled with his drink,
And this destroy'd him; for the wicked broth

> Confus'd the chemic labour of the blood,
> And tickling the brute brain within the man's
> Made havock among those tender cells . . .

Juvenal recalls the case of Caligula and the actual historical consequences of his wife's love philtre, which were so great that it was a happy stroke to invoke the thought: what would have happened to the world if Aphrodite's gift to Hera had made Zeus not mad with love, but mad indeed? This is the second larger-than-life image which is preparing the final climax of the poem. But Juvenal with a fine stroke cuts it off with a contrary historical reference: the poisoning of Claudius, which sent the trembling head of the Emperor, not to hell, but to godhead in the sky—a slavering godhead:

> et longa manantia labra saliua.

Now at last Juvenal, as it were, opens his throttle as he makes his last transition from magic to poison. He turns to children who have lost the protection of their fathers and, addressing them directly, warns them not to touch the food set before them by their mothers:

> liuida materno feruent adipata ueneno.

That Juvenal was both highly conscious of the effect he was producing and confident of carrying off his hyperbole in the face of irony is shown by his deliberate challenge to himself:

is this going beyond the laws of satire, am I straying into the incredible world of Greek fiction beloved of our modern tragedians, have I lost touch with Roman reality?

Juvenal now reveals why he has evoked the classical precedents of mothers murdering their children. It is to distinguish crimes of passion from cold-blooded murder whose motive is to secure the cash. Here Juvenal reinforces his brief

> sed
>
> non propter nummos

with a piece of natural imagery to bring home the distinction between spontaneity and deliberate calculation. Here there is no mockery of epic or merely literary connoisseuring of natural

beauty. The image, coming where it does, is strikingly like the
following from Donne's third satire:

> As streames are, Power is; those blest flowers that dwell
> At the rough streames calme head, thrive and do well,
> But having left their roots, and themselves given
> To the streames tyrannous rage, alas, are driven
> Through mills, and rockes, and woods, and at last, almost
> Consum'd in going, in the sea are lost:
> So perish Soules . . .

> quotiens facit ira nocentes
> hunc sexum et rabie iecur incendente feruntur
> praecipites, ut saxa iugis abrupta, quibus mons
> subtrahitur cliuoque latus pendente recedit.

The Latin in its way is doing dramatically what it is telling us
about. Juvenal need not be ashamed of comparison with Virgil:

> ac ueluti montis saxum de uertice praeceps
> cum ruit, auolsum uento, seu turbidus imber
> proluit aut annis soluit sublapsa uetustas,
> fertur in abruptum magno mons improbus actu,
> exsultatque solo, siluas armenta uirosque
> inuoluens secum . . .

which is slightly arty—or so it seems to me, and less inwardly
dramatic. Juvenal's point, however, is exactly that made by
Naevolus in the ninth poem. After the rush of this imagery we
have:

> illam ego non tulerim, quae conputat et scelus ingens
> sana facit . . .

Because of the indecency of the subject, I did not quote the central
charge Naevolus makes against his patron, but it must now be
given: it is of cold-blooded calculation:

> computat et ceuet.

This, at first sight, startling confrontation of texts works in two
ways, for it makes us wish to qualify both our account of Juvenal's detachment and of his seriousness. What, we may ask, has
this tremendous poem led up to? The final charge neither casts a
retrospective light on or sums up the whole of what has gone
before, nor does it prevent Juvenal ending the poem, as he did

the ninth, with a literary joke: 'The modern Clytaemnestra uses more subtle weapons that a two-handled axe, but will resort to cold steel if her Agamemnon has taken the precaution of dosing himself with the antidotes of Mithridates.'

Looking back over the final section, I cannot feel that we have any right to posit deadly earnestness anywhere, save in Juvenal's determination to get his effects right. For we are not made concerned primarily (or at all) to penetrate to Juvenal's own feelings. We are made to report on our own experience without rejecting any particle of it as we move under Juvenal's direction from the harmless if silly superstitions to the downright crimes. Yet we are not made to keep too vividly in our minds what we know either of Roman conditions or of the permanent features of human nature. Juvenal, of course, cannot quite fly in the face of the facts of either sort, but we cannot praise him for his closeness to the facts. His whole style keeps us at a distance from them—in many instances fortunately for our delicacy. Certainly, there are moments in this poem when a truth emerges: we feel that, for instance, religion *is* outraged, that cold, premeditated crime *is* less excusable than crime of passion, but we do not feel these things with any new depth or with greater precision.

The well-disposed reader, yet inclined at this point to accuse me of literary *escamotage*, of obtaining plausibility by an artful selection from the poem, might well challenge me to apply the above commentary to lines 286–345. Certainly, this passage begins with a re-statement of the opening theme of the poem, and this time the tone appears to be level and serious. If we cannot imagine Juvenal thanking Victor Hugo for his efforts to rehabilitate the Roman poet, yet we might fancy him making an exception for these lines from *L'année terrible, janvier* 1871, *Lettre à une femme*:

> Ce qui fit la beauté des Romaines antiques,
> C'étaient leurs humbles toits, leurs vertus domestiques,
> Leurs doigts que l'âpre laine avait faits noirs et durs,
> Leurs courts sommeils, leur calme, Annibal près des murs,
> Et leurs maris debout sur la porte Colline . . .

as catching the spirit of

> praestabat castas humilis fortuna Latinas

> quondam, nec uitiis contingi parua sinebant
> tecta labor somnique breues et uellere Tusco
> uexatae duraeque manus ac proximus urbi
> Hannibal et stantes Collina turre mariti.

But surely what makes the French—and Hugo, of all poets,—here superior to the English versions is that the Latin is *rhetorical* in the very best sense. We may see this, if we continue the quotation to its climax: *pax Romana* breaks the spirit more than a victorious army oppressing Italy:

> nunc patimur longae pacis mala, saeuior armis
> luxuria incubuit uictumque ulciscitur orbem.

Secondly, what matters is not that this remark would be endorsed by students of Roman society and civilization, but what Juvenal does with the thought in his poem. At first he merely restates his theme:

> nullum crimen abest facinusque libidinis, ex quo
> paupertas Romana perit . . .

Yet what follows? A vivid description of the consequences of heavy drinking and exciting food on the women of the upper classes. We must therefore consider the spirit of the following passage, for that will determine how seriously we take the mere letter of the summary of the causes of Roman degeneration.

Far from being hysterical or disorderly, Juvenal seems to me to exhibit perfect control. He remains quite detached and even cynically indifferent in the midst of the wild behaviour he is presenting. In fact his cold-blooded commentary turns what might have become a formidable *Walpurgisnacht* into mere Roman rhetoric. A second controlling factor is the male humour we know from Martial. For instance, by borrowing the following joke from Martial, or rather, by trying to outdo a piece of hyperbole that (one might have thought) would be the last word on the subject—Martial in 6.71 is describing the professional not the amateur, the public not the private, display of indecent and suggestive female postures:—

> tendere quae tremulum Pelian Hecubaeque maritum
> posset ad Hectoreos sollicitare rogos

Juvenal detaches us as male spectators from any tendency either to participate in the female orgy or to fly from it in exaggerated horror. The cool epic language and the absence of suggestive words—though if I fully understood Housman's note on this line, I suppose *hirnea* would have to be excepted—reinforce the effect:

> omnia fient
> ad uerum, quibus incendi iam frigidus aeuo
> Laomedontiades et Nestoris hirnea possit.

This Roman male humour comes out more strongly in the description of Clodius in lines 335–345, which refutes Naevolus' boast of *legitimum* and *longi mensura incognita nerui* by a stroke that makes one wish—as so often on this topic—to reduce 'male' to 'adolescent male'. Cicero had written an encomium on Cato which had cost Caesar great pains to refute: he had even been driven to issue two books, which, rolled into one, would look disproportionately large in the library if placed alongside Cicero's, and so give rise to the sort of joke Juvenal and Martial and his world enjoyed. (Compare, in this poem:

> testiculos, postquam coeperunt esse bilibres.)

This literary addition to the joke suggests that if we retain 'adolescent' as the word for the humour, we must think of the grown-up variety we find in the works of James Joyce, for the learned commentators go on to point out that if we consult the *chronique scandaleuse* of the period, we find that Juvenal is proposing quite an elaborate exercise in anthropometry, for what Clodius did to Caesar's honour, Caesar had done to Cato's, and therefore . . . but enough of this. For us it is more important to catch the humour in the contrasted ending of the two lines, one long and magniloquent, and the following, short and comical:

> Caesaris Anticatones

with the line that is bound to remind us of Horace:

> testiculi sibi conscius unde fugit mus,

which raises the merely schoolboy point to the level of literary wit. It does so, however, at the cost of blowing away all serious thought that might have been gathering in the preceding lines, so that when the passage ends with *ad quas non Clodius aras?* I feel that we are back again in the ninth poem:

> nam quo non prostat femina templo?

Where I most deplore the imputation of hysteria to Juvenal is where it tends to obscure a stroke of art which I think was meant to be centrally prominent in this central passage in the poem. It is the point where Juvenal returns explicitly to the goddess Pudicitia. He imagines a group of aristocratic women, including the Maura we have met before, returning in their litters from a party where the drinking had been exceptionally heavy, and as they pass the altar of the goddess, hitting on a means of relieving both their anti-religious feelings and their bladders, and thus freeing themselves for a moonlight orgy before they retire to their several palaces. Here Juvenal is far from cool, yet at no point hysterical. He begins with an *i nunc et* sneer to the husband, and his fierceness is all against the *sanna* (taken from Persius, the sneer that disfigures the whole face) and the words that pass between the women before the altar of Pudicitia. Juvenal's feeling about the episode is seen in the cold daylight an hour or so later, when the husband sets out in his correct court dress to begin his morning round of calls on the great, and soils his ceremonial shoes in the puddle before the altar:

> tu calcas luce reuersa
> coniugis urinam magnos uisurus amicos.

As this passage might very conveniently be made a touchstone of Juvenal's art in this poem—for the movement from 'hot', as it were, to 'cold' is just that, as we have seen, of the final climax of the poem—it will be well to pause over it for a moment. The wit is clearly obtained by compression: it would evaporate if the passage were expanded into prose. In that sense the wit is verbal. Yet it is as clearly not merely verbal, for there would be no wit at all if there were no given situation with its contrasted features. But if we ask what the compression focuses our attention on, it is surely more on the elements of the situation than on their bearing. If we call it predominantly visual wit, we do it no essential wrong, though, of course, it is more than that: the nose, the ears, have also been given material; so has the mind. But what seems to be totally withdrawn from the centre of our attention is the supposedly hysterical author. The firm placing of every word leaves no room for such mental wandering as would consider him: the language shackles us to the scene. Yet if we ask *what* the mind is given to work on, we must surely agree that Juvenal keeps to the surface, and that his art triumphs in *remaining external*.

External, certainly if we take as our touchstone one of the outbursts against women to be found in Shakespeare's plays. Let the reader for instance, after living over lines 314–334, turn to this:

> . . . The wren goes too't, and the small gilded Flie
> Do's letcher in my sight. Let Copulation thrive:
> For *Glosters* Bastard Son was kinder to his Father
> Than my Daughters got 'tween the lawful sheets.
> Too't Luxury pell mell, for I lack Souldiers.

Behold yon simpring Dame, whose face between her Forks presages Snow; that minces Vertue, and do's shake the head to hear of pleasures name. The Fitchew, nor the soyled Horse goes too't with a more riotous appetite: down from the waste they are centaures, though women all above: but to the Girdle do the gods inherit, beneath is all the fiends. There's hell, there's darkness, there is the sulphurous pit, burning, scalding, stench, consumption: Fie, fie, fie; pah, pah: Give me an Ounce of Civet; good Apothecary sweeten my imagination:

We could, I suppose, find a sense in which both passages might be defined as satires on women, yet if we compare Lear's remark on the divided nature of the sex with Pope's:

> A very Heathen in the carnal part,
> Yet still a sad, good Christian at her heart.

it at once becomes clear that Lear's apparent statements function rather, along with the rest, as giving us one man's shocked feelings about women rather than an appeal to the reader's judgement of the truth of the matter. By contrast Juvenal appears to be almost exclusively concerned to present a scene. And what a contrast! We may put it one way by asking what knowledge is required to enter imaginatively into each passage. For the Shakespeare, we need to have lived on a farm as well as in a respectable family. To appreciate Juvenal—I gather from the commentators—you would have had to visit a specialized brothel as well as the mime.

Yet when we ask, which is the more disturbing, it becomes clear that Juvenal is merely scandalous: we are invited to picture a scene which in real life, Juvenal says, would arouse only carnal passions. Lear invites us to see Hell on earth, and this in the unsensational, unspecialized, the pure lust of the flesh. Lear, that is, here invites us to generate out of our own hearts—given, of course, the crowded signals of the play—a horror latent under a respectable surface. Juvenal makes no such appeal: he is not interested in lust as it presents itself to the individual conscience as a soiling constituent of life. It is this *absence of interest* that is horrifying in Juvenal, and his success as a master of wit depends on the absence of any such reference within.

Here, with a self-reproaching *lusisti, iam satis est*, I close my remarks to the beginner, who can be assured that, while he will find the wit constantly present, the other poems of Juvenal are as different from each other as those I have here chosen to set him, as it were, on course. I shall be lucky if he has not blamed me for my prolixity. The expository critic nowadays tends to lose good manners and place his opaque body in front of the picture he is supposed to be revealing: since he can never feel sure of being understood *à demi-mot*, he usually gives two words where one might do. But in turning to my fellow amateurs, I feel reluctant to end here, and would wish to take leave with Martial's farewell to his fourth book:

> ohe, iam satis est, ohe, libelle.
> iam peruenimus usque ad umbilicos:
> tu procedere adhuc et ire quaeris,
> nec summa potes in schida teneri,
> sic tamquam tibi res peracta non sit,
> quae prima quoque pagina peracta est . . .

Whereas it would be a bold man who would say what the *potential* public for Juvenal is in 1963, those who already enjoy him understand each other and to some extent sympathize with and respect each other. It would therefore be an equal breach of good manners to part from those I have taken as my opponents without some reference to what would be their first objection to my counter-argument. A friendly 'classic' who, caring for Juvenal, had the patience to read through an earlier draft of this essay, brought an objection which, if valid, would ruin my whole thesis. He said, in effect: 'Yes, you have in this and that respect made out your case well enough, but you overlook the fact that your introduction to Juvenal cannot possibly stand, since it flagrantly contradicts in at least one vital point the introduction that Juvenal himself wrote to his poems. For what on your account becomes of *facit indignatio uersum*?'

To this my general answer would be on the lines of 'never trust the artist, trust the tale'. If the essential characteristics of Juvenal's art are as I have attempted to sketch them in considering these four poems, it does not matter much what Juvenal *says* about his aims and intentions in an introduction. But my particular answer would be that the first poem, so far from serving as an admirable introduction for the beginner, or giving the clue to the critic, itself requires an introduction, and bristles with difficulties of several sorts. One sort may be seen if we look at J. D. Duff's edition of Fourteen Satires of Juvenal and read where it occurs the following extract from an article by Nettleship, which may remind the reader of Bridges' introduction to the poems of Hopkins:

The first satire is a series of incoherent complaints. . . . A married impotent, an athletic lady, a barber rich enough to challenge the fortunes of all the patricians: the Egyptian Crispinus with his ring, the lawyer Matho in his litter: the infamous will-hunter, the robber of his ward, the plunderer of the provinces: the pandar husband, the low-born spendthrift, the forger, the poisoner; all these are hurried together in no intelligible order, and with the same introductory *cum hoc fiat*, and the same conclusion in several variations, *non scribam saturam*? Then at 1.81 the satire seems to open again and promise a description of various vices; but instead of this we have an elaborate complaint, extending over many lines, of the poverty of the nobility, with a description of the hardships of a client. . . . The ill-proportioned piece concludes with a promise to write against the dead.

Now, if anything is certain, it is that Juvenal would never have placed this poem at the head of the others if he had thought it open to these objections. We must therefore ask whether Nettleship was looking for the wrong things or whether what is extant is the poem as Juvenal wrote it. In any case, an attempt must be made to show how the extant lines ought to be taken.

I think my classical friend was right in supposing that the first poem was meant to serve as an introduction to the others and to set out Juvenal's claims to be regarded as a poet. But, in so far as I understand the poem, it seems to me to be more concerned with art than with its apparent subject-matter. If so, it gives me one last opportunity to argue with those who see Juvenal as the helpless victim of passion and passion arising from thoughts about the moral and social conditions of his age. If the poem, that is to say, had not its own special difficulties, and had been an acknowledged triumph, I should have welcomed the chance to challenge the view that Juvenal is a moral satirist on the evidence of these lines as much as on any others in his *œuvre*. My tactics, however, in this case, will be to try to say what the poem *is* before saying what it is not: that is, although I shall argue that Juvenal's *tone* tells us with what irony we should read *facit indignatio uersum*, I shall first attempt to establish its genre.

If it is a golden rule when we wish to appreciate what is inimitable in Juvenal to ignore the invitations of the commentators to look up a host of parallel passages which are *not* parallels, so it is a wise maxim, when Juvenal is being literary, to go as deeply into the literary tradition as the commentators can plunge us. We are in general apt to overlook the extent to which Latin poets were steeped in literature. Our excuse is in part the disappearance of the literature they were steeped in. Juvenal, I would claim, was as steeped in literature, carried as many of other poets' lines in his head as Chaucer, Dante, Milton, or Eliot, and he must have expected, since so many of his strokes of wit are parodies or criticisms of other poets, an audience equally steeped in the literature of the present and the past.

At any rate, this first poem seems to be consciously modelled on and challenging comparison with all the other *exordia* Juvenal knew of. That this is so, a brief glance will confirm. But once we admit the point, then the first chief puzzles arises: why if it was following the literary models so closely does it not conform to *all* the conventional requirements of the genre? Could it be that Juvenal saw himself as in some respects eccentric to the great Roman tradition? Is it possible in arguing that Juvenal is not a classical satirist to bring Juvenal himself into the witness box?

The amateur will, I hope, be pardoned for resorting to *moyens de fortune* in his attempt to demonstrate that the language used by Juvenal in this first poem is that conventional or even *de rigueur* for a poetic *exordium*. There may be more striking instances in the extant literature, but the one that comes to mind first is in the second book of Ovid's *Fasti*, where the author, like Juvenal, is making a solemn opening, in the spirit of

Begin, and somewhat loudly sweep the string.

Compare, for instance, the language of lines 149–150 in Juvenal's poem:

> utere uelis,
> totos pande sinus!

with this, from Ovid:

> nunc primum uelis, elegi, maioribus itis . . .

and lines 168–170:

> tecum prius ergo uoluta
> haec animo ante tubas: galeatum sero duelli
> paenitet

with the similar use of a military metaphor for literary activity in Ovid:

> haec mea militia est: ferimus quae possumus arma . . .
> nec galea tegimur . . .

For the image from horse racing in lines 19–20:

> cur tamen hoc potius libeat decurrere campo,
> per quem magnus equos Auruncae flexit alumnus

we have to turn to the almost identical *exordium* to Ovid's fourth book:

> nunc teritur nostris area maior equis.

The polite bespeaking of attention is almost identical, too. Juvenal wrote:

> si uacat ac placidi rationem admittitis, edam.

which resembles Ovid closely:

> ergo ades, et placido paulum mea munera uultu
> respice, pacando si quid ab hoste uacas.

If by a little extended research we confirm the fact that Juvenal is here attempting to rival his literary forbears in a conventional form, why, we may ask, are some features of the *exordium* missing from his poem? Why, to take a point that in isolation might seem unimportant, does Juvenal not follow the regular practice of *naming* the person or persons addressed? Why has he given no subject in line 21 to *admittitis*? A second regular feature, the permitted self-reference, is not altogether absent from Juvenal's poem, but if we compare it with the scope taken by Juvenal's

predecessors among the satirists, we may say that it is quite in-
sufficient. For to make satire acceptable the author must claim
to speak for the better part of the public; the poet, that is to say,
was expected to come forward and define his place in society in
such a way as to justify his attacks on it. So Horace, in the first
poem of his second book, wrote lines 74–77:

> quicquid sum ego, quamuis
> infra Lucili censum ingeniumque, tamen me
> cum magnis uixisse inuita fatebitur usque
> inuidia . . .

To this it is not a complete answer to say that Juvenal could
make no such claim since he clearly had never moved in the best
circles and had obtained his evidence about scandals in high life
from the Roman equivalent of the Sunday newspapers, the gossip of servants. I do not know in what circles Juvenal moved, but
if not in the highest, it was still open to him to follow Persius
and base his claim to write satire on his moral centrality derived
from a decent upbringing, as may be seen from the lines that
meant so much to Dryden that they came back to him when he
was writing on the young satirist, Oldham:

> When first my Childish Robe resign'd the charge;
> And left me, unconfin'd, to live at large;
> When now my golden *Bulla* (hung on high
> To House-hold Gods) declar'd me past a Boy;
> And my white Shield proclaim'd my Liberty;
> When with my wild Companions, I could rowl
> From Street to Street, and sin without controul;
> Just at that Age, when Manhood set me free,
> I then depos'd my self, and left the Reins to thee.
> On thy wise Bosom I repos'd my Head;
> And by my better *Socrates* was bred.
> Then, thy streight Rule set Virtue in my sight,
> The crooked Line reforming by the right.
> My Reason took the bent of thy Command,
> Was form'd and polish'd by thy skilful hand:
> Long Summer-days thy Precepts I reherse;
> And Winter-nights were short in our converse:
> One was our Labour, one was our Repose;
> One frugal Supper did our Studies close.
>   Sure on our Birth some friendly Planet shone:
> And, as our Souls, our Horoscope was one . . .

It is a poor equivalent for this to find as the only personal reference in Juvenal's poem:

> et nos ergo manum ferulae subduximus, et nos
> consilium dedimus Sullae priuatus ut altum
> dormiret . . .

> Provok'd by these Incorrigible Fools,
> I left declaiming in pedantick Schools;
> Where, with Men-boys, I strove to get Renown,
> Advising *Sylla* to a private Gown.

Not too much, perhaps, should be made of this; but taken with another feature also missing from Juvenal, it must arouse surprise. The Roman poets were expected to set out in their *exordia* their claim to originality, as Virgil did, for instance, in the third book of his *Georgics*:

> Thy fields, propitious Pales, I reherse;
> And sing thy Pastures in no vulgar Verse,
> Amphrysian Shepherd; the Lycaean Woods;
> Arcadia's flowry Plains, and pleasing Floods.
> All other Themes, that careless Minds invite,
> Are worn with use; unworthy me to write.
> Busiris Altars, and the dire Decrees
> Of hard Euristheus, ev'ry Reader sees:
> Hylas the Boy, Latona's erring Isle,
> And Pelops iv'ry Shoulder, and his Toyl
> For fair Hippodamé, with all the rest
> Of Grecian Tales, by Poets are exprest:
> New ways I must attempt, my groveling Name
> To raise aloft, and wing my flight to Fame.
> I, first of Romans, shall in Triumph come
> From conqu'red Greece . . .

Similarly, Horace (in the epistle from which Juvenal seems to have taken his first line:

> non ego, nobilium scriptorum auditor et ultor

had also said, in the words of the Loeb translator:

I was the first to plant free footsteps on a virgin soil; I walked not where others trod.

This boast could also be made in the deprecating '*qualiscumque*' formula familiar to us from the exordium to the poems of Catullus:

> quare habe tibi quidquid hoc libelli
> qualecumque; quod, o patrona uirgo,
> plus uno maneat perenne saeclo.

By modestly omitting the second limb of this plea, Juvenal has caused some of his readers to take him literally when he compared his own verses to those of Cluvienus:

> si natura negat, facit indignatio uersum
> qualemcumque potest, quales ego uel Cluvienus,

which is as absurd as to suppose that Dryden thought his own stuff as woeful as Shadwell's. Since therefore Juvenal might without offence have made as bold a claim as Catullus or Martial, we may wonder whether he was being genuinely modest when, in his seventh poem, he distinguished himself from

> uatem egregium, cui non sit publica uena,
> qui nihil expositum soleat deducere, nec qui
> communi feriat carmen triuiale moneta,
> hunc, qualem nequeo monstrare et sentio tantum . . .

the distinguished thing, the man whose line is out of the common, who never writes conventional stuff, who stamps each phrase with a note all his own,

> 'A man who does not exist,
> A man who is but a dream.'

But what most surprises me is that Juvenal did not seize the permission this opening poem gave him to discourse on a topic he must have known he had a right to speak about: the *style* which his form of poetry required. Both Horace and Persius seem to have enjoyed the chance to give us formulations such as this:

> est breuitate opus, ut currat sententia, neu se
> impediat uerbis lassas onerantibus auris;
> et sermone opus est modo tristi, saepe iocoso,
> defendente uicem modo rhetoris atque poetae,
> interdum urbani, parcentis uiribus atque
> extenuantis eas consulto. ridiculum acri
> fortius et melius magnas plerumque secat res.

You must be brief: strip from the theme the clogging verbiage, boring if too long-drawn-out: vary the tone from grave to gay, and try to alternate between the rhetorical style and that of easy, well-bred speech: do not insist; light mockery is often a more powerful means to reduce a topic to its right proportions than biting sarcasm . . .

Persius, too, on more than one occasion, offers us a formulation of the proper style for his poems, as here:

> C. uerba togae sequeris iunctura callidus acri,
> ore teres modico, pallentis radere mores
> doctus et ingenuo culpam defigere ludo.
> hinc trahe quae dicis mensasque relinque Mycenis
> cum capite et pedibus plebeiaque prandia noris.

> P. non equidem hoc studeo, pullatis ut mihi nugis
> pagina turgescat dare pondus idonea fumo.

> C. No, *your* style is based on good Roman talk
> made art by daring literary devices,
> full, but not fulsome: you expose the fault
> and scourge the pervert neatly with urbane wit.
> Take your themes from life and leave to tragedy
> fathers dining on joints of children's flesh:
> give us the meals real, common people eat.

> P. True, my aim is *not* to puff up solemn trifles,
> nor to weight my lines with stuff as light as smoke.

Still, these are sins of omission rather than commission, the reader will object, and, after all, Juvenal gave us a plain programme of the *scope* of his satire when he wrote:

> ex quo Deucalion nimbis tollentibus aequor
> nauigio montem ascendit sortesque poposcit
> paulatimque anima caluerunt mollia saxa
> et maribus nudas ostendit Pyrrha puellas,
> quidquid agunt homines, uotum timor ira uoluptas
> gaudia discursus, nostri farrago libelli est.
> et quando uberior uitiorum copia? quando . . . ?
> quando . . . ?

All that men have ever done since the time when the clouds absorbed the flood waters and Deucalion's ark made the ascent of Parnassus— when he consulted the oracle and hard stones slowly warmed and softened into living flesh and his wife could display naked girls to the males—man's wishes, fears, anger, pleasure, joys and general bustle and fuss, all this makes up the varied assortment of my book. And when was there a bigger bumper crop of vice and folly than nowadays? when . . . ? when . . . ?

But I am not the first to find this a misleading guide to the poems of Juvenal that follow. So great is the difficulty of taking this as an introduction that as long ago as 1920, E. Harrison, then of Trinity College, Cambridge, was bold enough to propose in Housman's presence that the lines 'quidquid agunt . . . libelli est' should be removed from the poem. 'Good and famous as the two lines are, I believe them to be out of place. They are in any case a strange description of Juvenal's matter. He is not a Balzac or a Dickens, but a man who looks for choice at the seamy side of life. Not prayers, fear, anger, pleasure, joys, and bustle are his theme, but selfish prayers, craven fear, wild anger, unwholesome pleasure, illicit joys, and feverish bustle.' Then why did not Juvenal say so, we may enquire, and the reply would be: 'he did. Remove the two lines, write *ecquando* for *et quando* and we have the familiar thought: no previous period of history could show a richer crop of vices than the present!' It is, however, a shocking thought to those who believe that Juvenal's text has come down to us comparatively unimpaired, if, just as the most famous line in the sixth poem:

> sed quis custodiet ipsos custodes?

so the best-known lines in the first—which Mayor used along with *facit indignatio uersum* to sum up the whole spirit of the thirteen poems of Juvenal he published his commentary on—should turn out to be homeless wanderers, no one knowing from what contexts they have been displaced!

When we recall the passage of Propertius mentioned above on page 136, we see that Juvenal stands in a witty Roman tradition. This first poem is among other things a witty attempt to rival Martial and Persius. Juvenal may not stand in the main satiric line of Lucilius and Horace, but he sides with those Roman poets who felt that the stock literary themes of epic, tragedy and elegy had exhausted their utility. One of Juvenal's starting-points may well have been that chosen by Martial in 10.4:

> qui legis Oedipoden caligantemque Thyesten,
>   Colchidas et Scyllas, quid nisi monstra legis?
> quid tibi raptus Hylas, quid Parthenopaeus et Attis,
>   quid tibi dormitor proderit Endymion?
> exutusue puer pinnis labentibus? aut qui
>   odit amatrices Hermaphroditus aquas?

which may be paraphrased:

What are you doing, Mamurra, with poems about the blind Greek, Oedipus, and the as-good-as blind Thyestes, Medea and her ilk, the two Scyllas (so often confounded by poets)? Confess, there never were such creatures on land or sea. What earthly good can you derive from impossible adventure stories for and about boys: Hylas' capture by the nymphs, Parthenopaeus, Attis or Endymion, whose capacity for dropping off to sleep produced such a fabulous sequel? What can you get from the legend of the flying boy and his forced landing in the 'drink', or from the other bonny lad who developed hydrophobia when he found what a pickle the all-too-close attentions of the water nymph had left him in?

Martial has peppered his target so generously that we cannot regard this epigram as directed exclusively against Statius. But the solemn parade of 'monsters' such as we find here came under Martial's fire:

> quid tibi monstra Erebi, Scyllas et inane furentis
> Centauros, solidoque intorta adamante Gigantum
> uincula et angustam centeni Aegaeonis umbram?
> . . . quis enim remeabile saxum,
> fallentisque lacus, Tityonque alimenta uolucrum
> et caligantem longis Ixiona gyris
> nesciat?

But when Martial continues, as we saw earlier:

> non hic Centauros, non Gorgonas Harpyiasque
> inuenies:

the suspicion arises that he may have aimed behind Statius at his master, Virgil:

> multaque praeterea uariarum monstra ferarum
> Centauri in foribus stabulant Scyllaeque biformes
> et centumgeminus Briareus ac belua Lernae,
> horrendum stridens, flammisque armata Chimaera,
> Gorgones Harpyiaeque et forma tricorporis umbrae.

In such an inclusive epigram there is no necessity to believe that when he mentioned Hylas or Scylla, Martial also had in mind Virgil's sixth eclogue. But that Juvenal was thinking of it is almost certain. He had already made use of it once, in his fourth poem, where he mocked the solemn invocation, *Pergite, Pierides*, that ushered in a number of these mythological monsters:

> narrate, puellae
> Pierides: prosit mihi uos dixisse puellas!

Tell on, Pierian virgins, and let it be put down to my credit that I call you virgins!

Now he seems to have fastened on these lines:

> hinc lapides Pyrrhae iactos, Saturnia regna,
> Caucasiasque refert uolucres furtumque Promethei:
> his adiungit, Hylan nautae quo fonte relictum
> clamassent, ut litus, Hyla, Hyla, omne sonaret.

If we knew in detail the literary discussions carried on in contemporary Rome, it might be worth making more of this 'anti-literary' bent. But even so, it would always be more important to stress the positive side, the claim that to be witty in Martial's way was to be closer to man and to life. The closeness of Juvenal to this and other epigrams of Martial in this first poem must surely be serving as a programme note to the public. To anticipate the discussion that follows I will put this note into words:

Dear readers, you have enjoyed Martial; now come and see whether I cannot give extra point to his favourite topics by setting them, as it were, to a different tune: the declaimer's mode. But I assume you understand what Martial was doing when he confined his poems to the conventional jokes of polite society. You will know then that to enjoy us you must both suspend and apply your critical and moral sense. We are not called on in our art to give you *all* the facts (you know them as well as we) or to assume all the moral attitudes (we are not moral censors) but to take those that allow the maximum witty play of the mind. Prepare yourselves, therefore, dear readers, to find in my poems all the butts of Martial's epigrams, and in particular, the comically obscene situations you enjoy so much in the mime. You will see from my rewritings of Martial that I have my own notes, particularly the sarcastic and the mock-tragic and epic, and that by fitting my sections together I can exhibit more attitudes to the same episode than you will find in any one of his epigrams. Nevertheless, and here I am thinking of the provinces, I take for granted that your copies of Martial have arrived safely and are well-thumbed, so that when I mention Rhodope or Chione you will know what I am getting at. (Also if you will look at the scansion of some of the proper names, you will see that I have

given some of Martial's figures slightly altered names.) Dear pro-
vincials, do not confuse your minds when you see us disporting ourselves as *Roman* wits. There is no need to suppose that we have lost
our heads or our morals. But life in the City is hard on persons like
ourselves who have no assured social position. You must therefore
expect to find us giving special prominence to one aspect of life as we
have known it, that of the respectable poor, dependent on our patrons,
and despised and displaced by the *nouveaux-riches*. Above all, do not
suppose that because we care supremely for the *lex* of our art, that we
care for nothing else; that I am *merely* declaiming because I treat my
themes with the cunning *désinvolture* I learnt from the rhetoricians.
Consult your Martial for the serious background to what in my poems
may superficially appear to be inconsistent fooling or rhetorical *pathos*,
etc.'

To support this reconstruction, to prove that it or something
like it is the point of the poem, I have to insist that the reworking
of Martial is so pointed as to force the reader to recall specific
epigrams. This will hardly be disputed in the case of 10.4. Compare, for instance, the reference to Hylas in both poems, the sarcastic treatment of Icarus:

> exutusue puer pinnis labentibus

with Juvenal's

> et mare percussum puero fabrumque uolantem

which, if we attend to the alliteration and the ablative, might be
rendered: 'the flying blacksmith and the plop when his son pierced
the surface of the sea.' And when we find in this epigram

> quid te uana iuuant miserae ludibria chartae?

may we not suppose that, although the topic was a commonplace,
Juvenal had this line in mind when he wrote:

> stulta est clementia, cum tot ubique
> uatibus occurras, periturae parcere chartae.

Cautiously following this clue, that when we find Juvenal
taking up topics or people who occur in Martial's poems we
should be on the look-out for a specific reference rather than
evidence that Juvenal and Martial lived in a world where these
and many other things were a common heritage (though we
should never exclude this latter consideration), we may wonder

whether Juvenal's Cluvienus is not Martial's Ligurinus. The *topos* of the poet who *will* recite is a commonplace, but if the reader will look up in Juvenal's first poem the words I have italicised in the following epigram (3.50), he may agree that a Roman reader might have made the specific reference:

> Haec tibi, non alia, est ad cenam causa uocandi,
>   uersiculos *recites* ut, Ligurine, tuos.
> deposui soleas, adfertur protinus *ingens*
>   inter lactucas oxygarumque *liber*:
> alter perlegitur, dum fercula prima morantur:
>   tertius est, nec adhuc mensa secunda uenit:
> et quartum recitas et quintum denique librum.
>   putidus est, *totiens si mihi ponis aprum.*
> quod si non scombris scelerata poemata donas,
>   cenabis solus iam, Ligurine, domi.

For our immediate purpose this can be glossed:

You invited me to a recitation of your rotten poems, not to a dinner, as I now know to my cost. For hardly had I drawn up to the table when you served a huge volume between the salad and the dressing. After this *hors d'oeuvre* (in both senses) you kept the first course waiting while you treated me to an unabridged hearing of a second volume. The interval between this course and the dessert gave you an opportunity to read out a third, a fourth, a fifth book. It is bad manners and worse taste to repeat the *pièce de résistance* so often in a meal. If you don't at once present the whole murderous library of your *opera* to the fish-and-chip man, you'll find yourself without a guest, Ligurinus, the next time you dine at home.

Similarly, if we concentrate in this first poem on the passages where Juvenal deals with Don Giovanni's vice, monophagy, or to replace it in its Roman context, *luxuriae sordes*, we may suspect that here again we are being referred, specifically referred, to Martial's epigrams on Caecilianus. To make my point I shall 'concoct' a passage from the poem:

> simplexne furor sestertia centum
> perdere et horrenti tunicam non reddere seruo?
> quis totidem erexit uillas, quis fercula septem
> secreto cenauit auus? sed quis ferat istas
> luxuriae sordes? quanta est gula quae sibi totos
> ponit apros, animal propter conuiuia natum?

poena tamen praesens; cum tu deponis amictus
turgidus et crudum pauonem in balnea portas,
ducitur iratis plaudendum funus amicis.

It passes the good, old-fashioned madness of our forbears to throw
away a fortune on cards while refusing a shivering servant a coat.
When did any of our ancestors build more houses than he could live
in or have seven-course dinners served when he dined alone? Who
can tolerate the thought of such meanness combined with such
wealth? Or imagine the greed of a man who could eat a whole boar
by himself—an animal born to create a full table to eat it? But such
excesses bring speedy punishment. Eat your peacock, strip, and try to
recover by a hot bath, and your coffin will be carried through the
streets amid the cheers of the friends you 'forgot' to invite to share the
delicacy with you.

If this had been the text presented to Juvenal's contemporaries,
it might well have seemed to them a connected whole, for the
commentators quote parallel passages showing that to Pliny and
Seneca the normal exemplification of *luxuriae sordes* was the abuse
of hospitality, the distinction between the meals served to friends
and those to poor hangers-on, or eating alone. The 'tragic'
conclusion might be taken as an instance to illustrate the superior
economy and rapidity of Juvenal, particularly if he were deliberately comparing himself with Persius:

> turgidus his epulis atque albo uentre lauatur,
> gutture sulpureas lente exhalante mefites.
> sed tremor inter uina subit calidumque trientem
> excutit e manibus, dentes crepuere retecti,
> uncta cadunt laxis tunc pulmentaria labris.
> hinc tuba, candelae, tandemque beatulus alto
> conpositus lecto crassisque lutatus amomis
> in portam rigidas calces extendit. at illum
> hesterni capite induto subiere Quirites.

> The laughing Sot, like all unthinking Men,
> Baths and gets Drunk; then Baths and Drinks again:
> His Throat half throtled with Corrupted Fleam,
> And breathing through his Jaws a belching steam:
> Amidst his Cups with fainting shiv'ring seiz'd,
> His Limbs dis-jointed, and all o're diseas'd,
> His hand refuses to sustain the bowl: ⎱
> And his Teeth chatter, and his Eye-balls rowl: ⎰
> Till, with his Meat, he vomits out his Soul: ⎰

Then, Trumpets, Torches, and a tedious Crew
Of Hireling Mourners, for his Funeral due.
Our Dear departed Brother lies in State,
His Heels stretch'd out, and pointing to the Gate: ⎫
And Slaves, now manumis'd, on their dead Master wait. ⎬
They hoyst him on the Bier, and deal the Dole; ⎭
And there's an end of a Luxurious Fool.

But the most striking evidence of its unity to Juvenal's audience would (I think) have been the fact that Martial himself had treated this complex of ideas in three epigrams about a figure who incorporated them, one Caecilianus. In 7.59 he is a man who dined alone on a boar:

> non cenat sine apro noster, Tite, Caecilianus.
>   bellum conuiuam Caecilianus habet.

Our friend Caecilianus always has a boar when he dines. He does not, Titus, dine with a bore.

Secondly, the whole movement of this 'passage' from Juvenal is present, from the madness to the death-wish, in 1.20:

> dic mihi, quis furor est? turba spectante uocata
>   solus boletos, Caeciliane, uoras.
> quid dignum tanto tibi uentre gulaque precabor?
>   boletum qualem Claudius edit, edas.

What madness is this, Caecilianus, tell me now, to invite a host of guests merely to see you wolfing down mushrooms? What prayer shall I formulate to equal in volume and intensity such a belly and such greed? It is that you might eat the kind of mushroom that Claudius ate.

I quote this epigram with the more confidence, since Juvenal had almost certainly just quoted it himself in the last poem he wrote before he composed this introductory piece. In the fifth poem, where he had been treating the same theme, and perhaps drawing on Martial's 3.60:

> sunt tibi boleti, fungos ego sumo suillos:

we find these lines:

> uilibus ancipites fungi ponentur amicis,
> boletus domino, set quales Claudius edit
> ante illum uxoris, post quem nihil amplius edit.

Champignons a wise man would look twice at before touching will

be served to the friends he treats like dirt. He himself will eat a mushroom equal in quality to the last Claudius tasted until his wife prepared
him an extra-special one—after which he gave up eating.

Thirdly, in the epigram (4.51) which may have given Juvenal
his *sexta ceruice feratur*, Martial used the same name, and may
have wished to associate the types, for the man who grows mean
as he grows rich.

Lastly, for I have no wish to be exhaustive, it seems to me
highly significant that when Juvenal calls up his *bête noire*, Crispinus, instead of drawing on his autobiography, he flies off to
another of Martial's epigrams. When we recall that *anuli* could
not appear in a hexameter, we must be struck by the closeness of

> nec sufferre queat maioris pondera gemmae

to both the words and situation of 11.37:

> anulus iste tuis fuerat modo cruribus aptus:
> non eadem digitis pondera conueniunt.

There is a difference between the light ring an *eques* wears on his finger
and the heavy ring a slave wears on his ankle. With your history,
Zoilus, you should not cause us to think of the latter when you wear
the former.

'But how does all this square with the last section of the poem?'
To this question I would have to answer that I do not know, but
also that I do not know how to make the section square with
anything in Juvenal. The primary difficulty in reading Juvenal is
to catch the tone, to fix the type of witty joke in each section;
as it were, how to interpret the expression on the poet's face.
Juvenal never speaks literally; when he is apparently poker-faced,
his is invariably a *pince-sans-rire*. So we hardly need the scholarly
information that his apparent statements are not facts: that at
the supposed time of composition there was comparative freedom
of speech: that Juvenal occasionally included the names of living
people (particularly those of his literary enemies in Pliny's circle).
But since I do not see the precise point he is making here, I am
obliged to interpret this section in the light of Juvenal's *practice*
in this and all his other poems.

If we wish to understand Juvenal it is important to see that his cases are all *notissima exempla*, yet in a rather special sense: they would all be given headlines in a sensational newspaper, or, to put it in another way, they are all candidates for caricature rather than character analysis. They are all very much larger than the human norm the moralist is properly concerned with. Juvenal wrote:

> aude aliquid breuibus Gyaris et carcere dignum,
> si uis esse aliquid.

> Wou'dst thou to Honours and Preferments climb,
> Be bold in Mischief, dare some mighty Crime,
> Which Dungeons, Death, or Banishment deserves.

lines which we should take closely with these from his sixth poem:

> inde fides artis, sonuit si dextera ferro
> laeuaque, si longe castrorum in carcere mansit:
> nemo mathematicus genium indemnatus habebit,
> sed qui paene perit, cui uix in Cyclada mitti
> contigit et parua tandem caruisse Seripho.

The astrologer owes his reputation nowadays to his having had the handcuffs on, to the time 'done' in a concentration camp in farthest Siberia. To be considered a *genius*, he must have received the death sentence, been reprieved at the last minute, and have suffered deportation to a penal settlement or come very near to detention at Her Majesty's pleasure.

These, we may say without much fear of exaggeration, are also the qualifications for mention in Juvenal's poems: which means that the cases Juvenal is most interested in treating are offered rather to our love of sensation, to our immediate enjoyment as spectacles, than to our sense of their intrinsic wickedness or to our feeling of their relevance to our own sins.

And this is where Juvenal's difficulties, were he to try to present a coherent positive moral programme, would begin. He would be in the embarrassing position the editor of a Sunday newspaper would find himself in, if, after weeks of pandering to the supposed public demand for pornography, he should launch a 'campaign against Vice'. The editor's embarrassment would be doubled if, under the plea of the libel laws, instead of handling the petty, humdrum forms vice actually assumes in modern life, he treated the public to all the *causes célèbres* of the last century.

The sceptical reader would be bound to ask: what is he doing this *for*? To a similar question Juvenal would not be able to present a clear, open answer. If this had been a polemical essay, instead of taking the poems in which Juvenal's claims to be a serious moralist appear strongest, I should have turned to the *locus classicus* for Juvenal's moral incoherence, his thirteenth poem, for there he is competing directly with the moralists in the form of a *consolatio*. That poem contains many isolated phrases, and some short passages, which in a better context could be used by a moralist. But the spirit of the whole poem reveals Juvenal's total failure to give a convincing picture of the moral temper. I therefore reject as bogus Juvenal's claim for Lucilius:

> ense uelut stricto quotiens Lucilius ardens
> infremuit, rubet auditor cui frigida mens est
> criminibus, tacita sudant praecordia culpa.

> But when *Lucilius* brandishes his Pen,
> And flashes in the face of Guilty Men,
> A cold Sweat stands in drops on ev'ry part:

by a quotation from that poem:

> quando recepit
> eiectum semel attrita de fronte ruborem?

> They, who have once thrown Shame, and Conscience by,
> Ne'er after make a stop in Villany.

If this be granted, we may take the meaning of

> experiar quid concedatur in illos
> quorum Flaminia tegitur cinis atque Latina

not as being, 'I shall carry out the traditional tasks of moral satire, but use the names of the safely dead', but 'out of notorious examples taken chiefly from the past, I shall make an original kind of great poetry'. This he has done in snatches of this first poem. At least I would class the following among the most rhythmically convincing passages Juvenal has left us:

> nam quis iniquae
> tam patiens urbis, tam ferreus, ut teneat se
> causidici noua cum ueniat lectica Mathonis
> plena ipso, post hunc magni delator amici

et cito rapturus de nobilitate comesa
quod superest, quem Massa timet, quem munere palpat
Carus et a trepido Thymele summissa Latino?

> To view so lewd a Town, and to refrain,
> What Hoops of Iron cou'd my Spleen contain!
> When pleading *Matho*, born abroad for Air,
> With his Fat Paunch fills his new fashion'd Chair,
> And after him the Wretch in Pomp convey'd,
> Whose Evidence his Lord and Friend betray'd,
> And but the wish'd Occasion does attend
> From the poor Nobles the last Spoils to rend,
> Whom ev'n Spies dread as their Superiour Fiend,
> And bribe with Presents, or, when Presents fail,
> They send their prostituted Wives for bail.

The poetry neither gains nor loses by our ignorance of the informer's name, by the possibility that all these figures never came
together historically, or by the remoter possibility that the audience could put contemporary names to *all* the personages and so
fit the passage exactly to an actual situation in Juvenal's day.

So obsessed have Juvenal's commentators become with the
view that he was writing with *saeua indignatio*, they overlook his
characteristic play of mind away from indignation at the close.
For, just as with the Crispinus portrait, Juvenal ends this section
with a joke. At least I take the reference to Latinus here as *not*
to his activities in private life as an informer under Domitian,
but to his activities on the stage, and imagine Juvenal is referring
to a comic episode from a mime in which he and Thymele were
the chief figures. But since this cannot be proved, I would rather
take a clearer example of this characteristic movement of Juvenal's
mind towards the witty aspect of the serious moral crime:

> cum leno accipiat moechi bona, si capiendi
> ius nullum uxori, doctus spectare lacunar,
> doctus et ad calicem uigilanti stertere naso?

> With what Impatience must the Muse behold
> The Wife by her procuring Husband sold?
> For though the Law makes Null th'Adulterer's Deed
> Of Lands to her, the Cuckold may succeed;
> Who his taught Eyes up to the Cieling throws,
> And sleeps all over but his wakeful Nose.

This needs no comment. It is humour again, if of a grimmer sort, that recalls us from melodrama, here:

> occurrit matrona potens, quae molle Calenum
> porrectura uiro miscet sitiente rubetam
> instituitque rudes melior Lucusta propinquas
> per famam et populum nigros efferre maritos.

> The Lady, next, requires a lashing Line,
> Who squeez'd a Toad into her Husband's Wine:
> So well the fashionable Med'cine thrives,
> That now 'tis Practis'd ev'n by Country Wives:
> Poys'ning without regard of Fame or Fear:
> And spotted Corps are frequent on the Bier.

Although it is clear that these passages are subdued to the witty stroke that closes them, we need not say that they are *sacrificed* to the wit, but we certainly lose the sense of a fixed attitude in the author, what we may call a moral standpoint. Juvenal does not offer anywhere the kind of coherence Nettleship looked for in vain. If anything is certain, it is that Juvenal as a poet did not hold any philosophic view which arranged the vices in a hierarchy and exhibited the relations between them. The instances of vice Juvenal gives us do not refer to any order either in his own mind or outside it. No doubt many of the cases do come under one of Juvenal's favourite heads: what sexual abominations people will commit for money, yet this does not exhaust his list. Juvenal discourages the moral cataloguer in us and sets us free to follow the varieties of his wit.

His tone in this poem is never monotonous. Anyone who can hear nothing but an uninterrupted shout of fury from beginning to end must be shutting his ears to the poetry. Many of the strokes are incompatible with *blind* passion: at every point the indignation is mixed with a different type of wit. For instance:

> atque triumphales, inter quas ausus habere
> nescio quis titulos Aegyptius atque Arabarches,
> cuius ad effigiem non tantum meiiere fas est.

Surely it is impossible to read the third line in the same tone we choose for the first two? Moreover, the variety of tones is what we have found characterizing the other poems. Can we read as a shout of fury or in the hissing voice required for

cum pars Niliacae plebis, cum uerna Canopi

the following piece of hyperbole:

> Frontonis platani conuolsaque marmora clamant
> semper et adsiduo ruptae lectore columnae.

You would think a bomb had hit Fronto's garden court from the havoc created by one persistent poet who *would* finish his epic recitation.

If we cannot feel how much air this lets into the poem, if we do not relish the advantages of the poet's *dédoublement*, we are bound to find Juvenal extremely nasty when he comes to these lines:

> cum te summoueant qui testamenta merentur
> noctibus, in caelum quos euehit optima summi
> nunc uia processus, uetulae uesica beatae?
> unciolam Proculeius habet, sed Gillo deuncem,
> partes quisque suas, ad mensuram inguinis heres.
> accipiat sane mercedem sanguinis et sic
> palleat ut nudis pressit qui calcibus anguem
> aut Lugdunensem rhetor dicturus ad aram.

We should certainly look askance at a Father of the Church who lashed this vice with such point! Surely it is relevant here to return to the remarks made earlier on the ninth poem? Although I have no intention of unravelling the imagery in the two similes for sexual *pallor*, they seem to me to be of the same type as the three chosen to illustrate the exhaustion of Naevolus.

Also making against any simple-minded account of Juvenal's feelings in this poem are the examples of declaimer's wit. When Juvenal asks

> quem patitur dormire nurus corruptor auarae?

my reply is: *incredulus odi*, and I class the line with similar lines in his second poem, such as

> quis caelum terris non misceat et mare caelo
> si fur displiceat Verri . . . ?

In fact it needs all the deflationary power of the wit in the next lines to bring me round to Juvenal's side:

> si natura negat, facit indignatio uersum
> qualemcumque potest, quales ego uel Cluuienus,

On looking back over this essay I must ruefully constate that its principal object has been sacrificed to its subordinate aims. 'Yes,' it may be said, 'we see the direction in which you are steering us, but the goal doesn't look very attractive; the prospect of pleasure seems very much less than that Dryden's remark promised. We, too, have enjoyed reading Eliot and Pound, but, surely, Juvenal's wit is something if not inferior yet very much more *specialized* than theirs?' A second objection might well be that some account of the laws of satire is required to make room for Juvenal's branch of witty satire. I am aware of having circumscribed rather than defined the wit. But there are limits to what can be undertaken even in an extended essay. I hope to have at least cleared the way for a consideration of what matters in Juvenal and of what may be made to matter to the modern reader. The next step—once we cease to look for the moralist and the social historian and to search the poems for autobiography—is to appreciate Juvenal as a *supreme manipulator of the Latin language*. Before comparing him with the satirists of the world, we need to compare him with the other Roman poets.

INDEX OF NAMES

INDEX OF PASSAGES